MAKE YOUR LIFE
A MASTERPIECE

MAKE YOUR LIFE A MASTERPIECE

Peter Legge
with
Tashon Ziara

EAGLET PUBLISHING

Eaglet Publishing
4th Floor, 4180 Lougheed Highway
Burnaby, British Columbia, V5C 6A7 Canada

Library and Archives Canada
Cataloguing in Publication

Legge, Peter, 1942-
    Make your life a masterpiece / Peter Legge with Tashon Ziara.

ISBN 0-9695447-8-2 (bound)
ISBN 0-9695447-9-0 (pbk.)

    1. Success. 2. Self-actualization (Psychology). I. Ziara,
Tashon. II. Title.
BF637.S8L4535 2006   158.1   C2006-900008-5

First Printing   April 2006

Jacket design by Catherine Mullaly
Typeset by Ina Bowerbank
Edited by Kim Mah
Printed and bound in Canada by Friesen Printers

Dedication

To my wife Kay
> *You continue to lift me to the mountaintop*

To my three daughters Samantha, Rebecca, Amanda
> *You are a father's greatest dream*

To Karen Foss, Neil Soper and Heather Parker
> *Your loyalty, devotion and commitment*
have formed the backbone of Canada Wide
Magazines & Communications Ltd.
> *I would have slipped off had you not brought*
balance to the pallet.

Other books by the Author

How to Soar With the Eagles
You Can If You Believe You Can
It Begins With A Dream
If Only I'd Said That
If Only I'd Said That, Vol. II
If Only I'd Said That, Vol. III
Who Dares Wins
The Runway of Life

Booklets
97 Tips on How to Do Business in Tough Times
97 Tips on Customer Service
97 Tips on How to Jumpstart Your Career

CD
The Runway of Life

ACKNOWLEDGEMENTS

As I reflect on my past 30 years as President of Canada Wide Magazines & Communications Ltd., it is impossible not to be grateful and appreciative of the dozens of very talented writers, art directors, accountants, sales executives and administrators who have given of their talents and expertise as our company has grown and flourished.

If we have one single claim to fame, it is that in those 30 years, we have never lost money, ever! Quite a feat. Is there a secret to our success? I don't believe so. Rather, there are three essential elements that contribute to the success of any business, and I will share them with you:

1. Always be ready to adapt to changes in and around your industry — understanding that these may occur on a weekly basis.

2. Treat your staff with great respect. Empower them to succeed and then get out of the way.

3. Stay focused on what you do best (for us, it is clearly magazines and related graphic services) and then build strong partnerships with complementary organizations in your chosen profession to deliver an unbeatable product or service.

In all three of these areas, I believe we have stayed true to our business, and this book is a reflection of that commitment. My deepest appreciation and heartfelt thanks go to the dedicated team at Canada Wide who were vital in the editing and production of this, my ninth book. They are a testament to the quality of staff throughout the company:

Kim Mah — A meticulous editor and proofreader; there is no one better.

Cathy Mullaly — The talented art director of *BCBusiness* magazine, who designed the dust jacket.

Ina Bowerbank — A master typesetter, infallible in her attention to detail.

Debbie Craig — An electronic imaging expert, who helped bring the cover photograph to life.

Corinne Smith — Our Vice President, Production, whose reputation for being on time and on budget is the hallmark of her success in a highly demanding job.

Dale Clarke — My tireless personal assistant, who approaches everything with an energetic, fun and serving attitude and manages to juggle my many and varied business, speaking and public service commitments effortlessly.

Tashon Ziara — My writer/editor/researcher, who spent many hours bringing to life my stories and experiences and applying the 30 principles we use at Canada Wide so that we could share them with other businesses, organizations, or indeed, anyone who endeavours to build a masterpiece of their own.

I have said before that no one makes it on their own — I didn't! Thank you, team, I am proud of every one of you.

Peter Legge
April 2006

TABLE OF CONTENTS

INTRODUCTION

Celebrating Milestones

The month of April 2006 marks the 30th anniversary of Canada Wide Magazines and Communications Ltd. and the 20th anniversary of my professional career as a keynote speaker.

Life is full of milestones that should be celebrated and this year is especially significant for our company given the fact that when I first started out to build Canada Wide Magazines — beginning with just one 10-cent publication called *TV Week Magazine* — more than a few people were placing bets on how long it would be before I went belly up. Rumour had it back then in 1976 that some people were wagering that the company wouldn't last six months. Others, who were a bit more optimistic, said it couldn't survive more than five years; still others suggested that the company might make it to 10 years if I were extremely lucky.

Betting aside, the consensus at the time seemed to be that there really wasn't a market for a locally produced weekly magazine whose main contents were TV listings. Add to that the fact that I had no business degree at the time (although last time I checked, sheer will and power of conviction aren't taught in business school), no previous experience in the magazine industry (or publishing of any kind for that matter), and there you had it — a failure just waiting to happen.

If everyone were right, I would be just another statistic, one of the 80 per cent of new businesses that fail within the first three to four years due to a lack of resources, financial liquidity or management experience. What no one was counting on back then was my determination to succeed. Although I agreed that the magazine, which I had purchased from radio station CKNW's colourful and bombastic sports director Al Davidson (commonly known as Big Al), had not flourished in its first few years of life, I definitely saw potential in the concept and knew that I had the salesmanship to make it both bigger and better.

The fact that I ended up buying this particular magazine is one of the funny coincidences of this story — although I really believe that there are no coincidences in life, just opportunities that we can choose to either act upon or walk by — because when Big Al originally started the forerunner of *TV Week* (it was called Al Davidson's *This Week Magazine* at that time), he approached me to be the general sales manager for the magazine. The main reason I declined his offer was that even back then, I realized that Big Al was a far better sportscaster than he was a businessman.

To his credit, Big Al did manage to keep the magazine going for a few years. However, by 1976 he had had enough; the enterprise was in receivership and so indebted to the printer that the printing company now controlled ownership of the magazine and was looking for someone to take over as publisher. That someone was me.

Today, Canada Wide Magazines is considered to be the largest independent magazine publisher in Western Canada, with 36 titles covering everything from business to gardening, golf to mining and architecture to travel. We still have *TV Week* magazine as well, and in terms of revenue it continues to be our flagship. Today it is run by my daughter Samantha, and I am proud to say that Sam is the third generation of our family to be involved with *TV Week* — both myself and my father have also taken a turn — and she does a better job than the two of us put together. This is no easy feat, given the complex business mix involved (the magazine's content has to appeal to both subscribers and newsstand purchasers) and the fact that we go head-to-head with a much larger, international TV listings publication that shall remain unnamed here.

The journey to where we are today has not always been an easy one. I remember when we had our 10th anniversary; we were still being plagued with questions about how long we would be in business. At that point, I realized that if we were ever going to be as big as I believed we could be, Canada Wide would have to squelch the perception people had that we could be squashed at any moment by the "big boys."

I sat down with the Canada Wide team to come up with a plan for something that would make a big impact in the community and announce to everyone that we had arrived. After all, we were a B.C. company that had been in business for a decade and we were determined to be here for many more decades to come.

Together, the plan we came up with was to take whatever profit we had accumulated up to that point and make a big splash to position ourselves as though we were infinitely more successful than we were at the time. The plan included an advertising campaign using local media personality Doc Harris, and a gala roast at the Bayshore Hotel — with yours truly on the menu as the main course — for every member of our staff and their spouses.

We also invited hundreds of our clients, the media and some special guests. We wanted to tell the world that we had arrived and we spent virtually 95 per cent of the profit we had at the time to put on this show. In addition, we took our really big clients — those who had been with us for a long time and essentially used their advertising dollars to invest in Canada Wide and *TV Week* — to Las Vegas for a weekend. Because our whole approach to business has always been built on personal relationships, these clients had gone to the wall for us and we wanted to let them know how much that meant to us.

I'm happy to say that the end result was exactly what we wanted; following our big splash, the market finally began to take us seriously as a company. In no short order, people stopped asking us when we were going out of business and started booking more advertising space in our publications and exploring other ways in which they could work with us (given that we were obviously capable of holding our own against the big boys).

It was at this point as well that I decided Canada Wide Magazines needed to continue to grow and build on its success. I therefore set a goal that the company should add one new magazine for each year that we are in business (we are presently ahead of schedule with 36 titles and 30 years of business).

It has taken a great deal of persistence, patience and a positive attitude to build Canada Wide Magazines to where it is today and I believe these three traits are the keys to my continued success. As a young salesman just starting out, my father gave me some good advice that I have kept front and centre during these past 30 years.

"No one makes it on their own, Peter," he told me. "You must develop a pleasing personality and the ability to get along with other men and women in every situation. When people like you, they want you to succeed."

My father's words were true, and this book is dedicated to the men and women who have contributed to Canada Wide Magazines along the way. In addition to sharing some stories about the 30-year journey that has brought us to where we are today, I would also like to pass along 30 important tools for success that have served me in the making of my own masterpiece. I trust that you will use them well.

PROLOGUE

Make Your Life a Masterpiece

"For what is the best choice for
each individual is the highest it is possible
for him to achieve."

— Aristotle

I'd like you to take a moment right now and think about what comes to mind when you hear the term "a masterpiece." Do you imagine some great classical work of art like Leonardo da Vinci's painting of Mona Lisa, Michelangelo's statue of David or Mozart's "Requiem"? Or perhaps the phrase makes you think of someone whom you believe has a rare talent or genius, like Thomas Edison with his invention of the light bulb, Albert Einstein with his *Theory of Relativity* or Henry Ford with his Model T motor car.

What is interesting about the concept of a masterpiece in the modern world is that we tend to think of it as the very best work that an individual could ever produce, the culmination of a life's work or the definitive magnum opus that cannot be topped; and yet, that is not the original meaning of the term.

By its original definition, a "master-piece" actually refers to a specific piece of work created by a journeyman (the next step above an apprentice) craftsman or artisan who aspires to become a master and gain admittance into a professional guild. Therefore, it is not the culmination of one's life's work, but rather a project undertaken to prove that as a journeyman, one has mastered the basic skills necessary to be considered qualified to practice his profession and offer his services under his own name.

For example, in centuries past (beginning in the Middle Ages), someone who had studied the art of fine furniture-making for a long time (approximately six years as an apprentice and three as a journeyman) would make one single piece, "a master-piece," in which he would bring together and demonstrate everything he had learned while working under the guidance of a master. The piece that he produced would often be a miniature version of an object that a master craftsman could be expected to make for a customer, a mechanical writing table, for example.

The purpose of the finished piece would be to show that the person who made it could choose woods correctly (and match different kinds of woods), enamel, engrave and deal with a variety of materials for decorative inlays such as metal, bone, amber and stone. It would also demonstrate that he had the highest technical skills in finishing and polishing and the greatest precision in all of the basics of his craft — the miniature dovetail joints would have to be flawless and any moving parts, such as drawers, hinges or clasps, would be expected to operate perfectly in every way.

For a journeyman, to build such an object would take a great deal of time and care, coupled with immense skill and indeed, mastery of all of the tools and materials of the trade. In fact, in many cases the journeyman would spend several months working on this "potential masterpiece" knowing that it would be shown to existing master craftsmen who would proceed to check it out most thoroughly, considering not only the aesthetic aspects of the object, but also the workmanship, right down to the smallest detail of each and every fitting and decoration. Then, only if the masters were satisfied in all ways as to the craftsmanship and the attention that had been afforded in the construction of the desk, would they declare it to be a masterpiece and accept the journeyman into the guild as a peer.

In this way, creating one's masterpiece was both an end and a beginning at the same time, for while it signalled that the journeyman's formal training was complete, it was also the point at which he would begin to be officially recognized for the work he produced. This is because up to the time when a craftsman or artisan achieved the rank of master, everything he produced would be credited to the master in whose shop he worked. Because of the large projects they were commissioned to do, some masters were known to have dozens of apprentices and journeymen working in their shop or studio, many of whom were content to earn a good wage year in and year out, with no interest in attempting to become a master.

To attempt to make a masterpiece and take one's life to the next level, regardless of the field of endeavour, was then, and still is today, an undertaking that requires courage. Without the practical and actual completion of our masterpiece, we may think or believe that we are as good as (or better than) the masters who taught us, but the proof is missing and without it we can never say that we have lived up to our full potential. Presentation of a masterpiece shows both a willingness to be critiqued by the best in our field and a desire to achieve a high standard of performance.

Finally, and perhaps most importantly, undertaking our masterpiece opens the door to a whole new world of personal exploration — for mastery is an individual journey — no longer are we indistinguishable from all of the other apprentices, but we are now free to set our own goals and challenges. That is what this book is about, choosing to be the master of one's own destiny. The master becomes the final authority on his own development, his own path and his own contribution.

It is in the decision to attempt a masterpiece that the transformation from journeyman to master really begins. It is a great challenge, to be sure, and one that many people will never feel ready to attempt. However, to know that such a challenge exists and to truly understand that we are free to rise to the test whenever we choose is both exciting and inspiring. I believe that we all have the potential to make our masterpiece — though what that is, is up to each one of us to determine for ourselves. I sincerely hope that within this book, you will find the tools you need to begin working on your own masterpiece!

CHAPTER 1

"To every man there comes in his lifetime
that special moment when he is
figuratively tapped on the shoulder and
offered a chance to do a very
special thing, unique to him and fitted
to his talents. What a tragedy if
that moment finds him unprepared or
unqualified for the work which
would be his finest hour."

— Winston Churchill

Masterpiece Tool:
Prepare Yourself for Success

My speaking career and annual engagements total, on average, about 100 occasions per year. The invitations I receive to address groups range from industry associations to credit unions, to real estate organizations, investment groups, hotels, car dealerships, provincial governments, conventions of all kinds and an assortment of rallies; in total, a very wide range of audiences.

The majority of my speeches centre on topics revolving around leadership and business success, and every speech is very heavy on motivation and inspiration with plenty of personal anecdotes and stories from my own experience and life in general.

Following almost every speech, these are the three most

common responses I receive from the men and women I speak to:

1. How do you make it look so easy?
2. I wish my children could have heard that talk.
3. I want to be a speaker just like you . . .

   I want to travel first class!

   I want to ride in a limo!

   I want to stay at five-star hotels!

   I want audiences to give me standing ovations!

   I want to be paid big bucks!

To those people who want to live my life, my rejoinder is always the same, "That's great! Now tell me, what are you prepared to do in order for that to happen?"

Not surprisingly, very few people have an answer for this question. No doubt they dream of being in "the business," that is, the business of being a well-paid public speaker. However, what they often fail to realize is that the speaking business is just that, a business, and the people who succeed are those who are willing to work hard, sacrifice and give it their all. Therefore, any secrets I can share on this aspect of my life can easily be adapted to just about any business venture. What people see when I am up on that stage in front of them is the end result of many years of hard work and dedication and a real passion for what I am doing.

CKNW radio broadcaster and *TV Week* writer Rick Forchuk once told me that I have paid the price to be successful and I agree, although I would add that I continue to pay the price to stay successful. This is a competitive business and I must continually add value to my presentations and keep my skills sharp.

This is where the proverbial rubber meets the road in almost every endeavour.

You see, there really are no secrets to being successful. You have the same time available to you as anyone else does. If you were to do the same things that other successful people in your profession do on a regular basis, with the same dedication, and learn the skills that are available to just about everyone, given enough time (this is the investment that all apprentices must make to one day become masters of their craft), you should be as successful as anyone else in your chosen field.

If I'm pressed on this issue of speaking and how I do what I do, I generally ask two simple questions, "What are you prepared to do in order to be a successful speaker?" and "What have you done in your past that has prepared you for this career, i.e., what do you think qualifies you for such a demanding job?"

Contrary to what some people might think, I wasn't born giving great presentations. Just like everyone else, I had to start at the bottom (as an apprentice) and learn my lessons — some of them the hard way — before I became a master of my craft.

Travel with me back to my hometown in England almost 50 years ago. It is Greenford, Middlesex, just after the Second World War, and I am 11 years old. It is the time before television sets begin to appear in every single household in the country, when the most popular form of entertainment besides BBC Radio programs like *The Goon Show* (which starred Peter Sellers, Harry Secombe and Spike Milligan) is the local cinema.

In Greenford, the theatre is called The Granada Cinema. Today, it has been replaced by a Tesco supermarket, but on my last visit it still resembled the old Granada Cinema with all its memories.

My grandfather was an usher at the theatre and he always looked splendid in the uniform that was supplied by the cinema. On his chest, he proudly displayed the medals that had been awarded to him for service to his country in the First World War.

I still have his medals, "presented to William Ashby by a grateful nation," mounted and proudly hanging on the wall in my home office.

On the days when he was working at the theatre, he would often spot me and his daughter (my mother) in the queue for a movie and by some sleight of hand let us into that day's show for free.

We were not a wealthy family by any means — although always happy — and we struggled like so many others at that time with post-war ration books and a limited supply of goods for sale. For this reason, my mother was always grateful for this gesture that allowed her to save a few pennies and still have a bit of entertainment during what was an otherwise dark time.

In those days, an afternoon's program consisted of two movies, along with a newsreel on world events, particularly those that affected Great Britain. Between the first and second movie, an organist would rise on a platform seemingly out of nowhere and play while a packed house would sing rousing British songs to cheer our spirits.

To my mind, it was a wonderful time to be a kid in England. Perhaps this is because I never saw our family as being poor. We were a close family and content to do whatever it took to make ends meet. And despite whatever hardship they themselves might have endured, my mother and father always provided for their one and only son — me!

One of the highlights of the week for us kids — especially during summer holidays — was the Saturday morning movie, which was only for youngsters. It went from 9 a.m. to noon and every Saturday the Granada was jam packed. Almost 1,500 kids crammed into the theatre to watch cartoons, a feature film (usually a western with Roy Rogers and Trigger), Tom Mix newsreels and a serial program to finish off the show (and keep you coming back week after week).

The whole morning cost just six pence (about 25 cents).

Maybe it was cheap babysitting for a war-torn country, and if so, it was certainly successful, as it kept our minds off what we didn't have. As always, about halfway through the show, the organist would pop up out of nowhere and 1,500 kids would sing the current favourite songs at the top of their lungs.

In our group of friends, we had about 20 or 25 kids who would regularly go to these Saturday morning movies and we loved them more than anything else in our week! So it was that on one Saturday, they called for a talent show from amongst the kids in the theatre. Three performers were to be selected from the audience and my friends encouraged me to try out. Thinking that it might be good for a laugh, I did and was selected to perform. The song I chose to sing was "Mr. Sandman" by The Chordettes.

So, for 1,500 screaming kids, I stood on stage for the very first time at the Granada Cinema and sang!

Was I any good?

I really have no idea.

My friends all said that I was, but alas, no recording contract ever arrived.

Nevertheless, as scary as that performance was for me, it was also exhilarating. Little did I know at the time that it would plant a seed in me that (while it would lie dormant for a number of years) would ultimately set me on a course and set in motion the desire to be in the entertainment business, and lay the groundwork for my life as a professional speaker.

I was in for the ride of my life.

———•·•———

What are some of your memories as a child of things you enjoyed doing that could have planted a seed and laid a foundation for your future?

How many of these have you pursued in your life?

Is there something you truly enjoyed when you were younger that you gave up and now regret not pursuing? Perhaps you could revisit it now?

———

Life for my mother and father in London, England, was tough — as it was for millions of people following the war. We had no phone, no television set, no central heating and very few "mod cons" as they liked to call modern conveniences. Money, careers and a future were very foreign concepts to my parents. In fact, Sunday dinners for us were always at my grandmother's house, where one of her permanent boarders was her brother Ernie Hammond.

Luckily for us, my Uncle Ernie worked as a butcher in Greenford High Street and at the end of each week he would have his pick of the roasts that not been sold to bring home for Sunday dinner. In those times of rationing, it was often the only meat we had all week — and I always knew that Monday night's meal would be shepherd's pie, made with the leftover meat from Sunday dinner.

It was 1953-54 and the future looked bleak. My father decided that he had had enough of scrimping and no saving. He and his family needed to emigrate somewhere to seek out a life and a country that, given enough hard work, commitment and dedication, would provide a brighter future. He thought of all the places he had visited in his younger years.

You see, when my father was 16 he ran away to sea, boarding a small freighter in the town of Barry, South Wales. The name of the ship was *Vancouver City*. In his time as a sailor, he circumnavigated the globe seven times and visited Vancouver, British Columbia, four times. So it was that when my mother asked where we should go, he was quick to answer, "Of all the ports I ever visited, Vancouver was the prettiest and my very first ship was named after that city, so let's go there." And that was it . . .

It's funny how some of life's biggest problems can be solved by a decision that was made in a heartbeat. I'm not sure my father had heard of William of Ockham, a British-born medieval philosopher who practised a method of problem-solving that has become known as "Ockham's Razor" (see more about Ockham in Chapter 8), but he applied the principle perfectly.

Ockham said, "The simplest and most direct resolution requiring the fewest number of steps is usually the correct solution to any problem."

As humans, we often make the mistake of overcomplicating both our problems and our goals. But the truth is, the more complicated the solution, the less likely it is ever to be implemented.

While researching and writing this book at our winter home in Palm Springs early in January 2006, we were playing golf at the Rancho Mirage Golf & Country Club and were teamed up with another couple our age, Derek and Janet Spooner. Somewhere around the third hole, we discovered that they too live in Vancouver, despite their distinctive accents that told us they were originally from England. In actual fact, Janet was born in South Wales, close to my father's hometown of Barry.

In the course of conversation, my wife asked them how they had decided to move to Vancouver. They told us that they had posed the following question to a friend living in England, "If you could emigrate anywhere in the world, where would you go?"

"Let me put it this way," the friend responded, "If I were to phone my wife and ask her 'How would you feel about moving to Vancouver, Canada?', she would be packed and ready to go before I got home."

So that's how the Spooners decided to come to Vancouver with two kids and a budgie. Talk about courageous. That was 30 years ago; they took a risk and became successful Canadians as a result.

A MASTER KNOWS: The secret of success in life is to be ready for opportunity when it comes.

Now, getting back to my family's story . . . following a quick visit to Canada House in London's Grosvenor Square and a bit of paperwork, we were on our way, although we never really made it to Vancouver. Instead, my parents settled in New Westminster, where I attended Vincent Massey Junior High School and then Lester Pearson High School — both schools named after giant Canadians, I might add.

It was here that I emceed a few pep rallies, performed at assemblies and really caught the show business bug. If you've ever seen TV shows like *Laverne & Shirley* or *Happy Days* (which are a pretty accurate depiction of life in the late '50s and early '60s), you'll know that high school in those days truly was a blast. However, as is inevitable, life became a little more serious once we graduated. We also realized that life wasn't as simple as it had been in high school; as young adults, we had to get jobs and begin fending for ourselves.

With the show business bug still in my system, I tried my hand at more performances. Fancying myself an up-and-coming comedian, I watched just about every comic who was on TV, studying their technique and material. Watching *The Ed Sullivan Show*, which was a Sunday night ritual, I dreamed of the day when it would be me in front of the cameras making everyone laugh.

After a few years of performing, an opportunity came my

way to entertain at the Marine Drive Golf and Country Club in Vancouver. In the audience was John Usher, the booking manager for the P&O Shipping Line. He liked what he saw and offered me a position onboard the *SS Oriana*, sailing from Vancouver to Southampton, England. I jumped at the opportunity, and after a teary farewell from my parents, set sail for my first big solo adventure.

My very first night on the ship, I met an enchanting young lady whom I would end up marrying six months later. Kay Tanner, who had grown up in England, had spent the previous year living in Seattle with her family while her father worked in the U.S. Now, she was returning to England to see the fiancé she had left behind and discover if there were still any sparks between them. I learned about Kay's engagement three or four days into the trip and realized that I would have to work fast if I wanted to have any chance at changing her mind.

On the dock in Jamaica — which was the last port of call before the transatlantic crossing that would take us to Lisbon, Cherbourg and then on to Southampton — I took fate into my own hands, asking Kay to write her fiancé and advise him that he needn't meet her at the dock when we landed.

"What are you going to do about it?" she asked me.

"I would like to marry you," I told her.

Luckily for me, she said yes. We have now been married for 37 years and counting. Looking back, I wasn't at all sure about where my future would lead me, but with the addition of my life partner, the picture on my canvas was beginning to take shape.

Now that I had a wife, I needed to get serious about my career. As you probably know, any career or business venture has its challenges at the beginning. Unless you are really dedicated, truly love what you are doing and are willing to pay your dues, chances are that you're not going to make it. The path that I took in the show business arena posed as many obstacles as you might want to encounter.

Andrew Carnegie once said, "The world needs men that have the courage to act on their own initiative. Moreover, men of this type write their own price tag and the world willingly pays it. The world willingly rewards men of initiative."

I wanted to be such a man and so, shortly after I arrived in England, I hooked up with Rolf Harris's agent. Rolf, by the way, got his big start at Ken Stouffer's Cave theatre restaurant in Vancouver. His agent's name was Phyllis Rounce and she booked me into theatres and nightclubs throughout Great Britain. So it was that just two weeks into our marriage, I kissed Kay goodbye and boarded a British Rail train to Southport (about 20 minutes from Blackpool) to head out on the club circuit. It wasn't a very glamorous life, to be sure. In those days, you would do one show on a Sunday afternoon, two shows per night Monday through Saturday and then travel the following Sunday to arrive at your next gig. We always stayed in very inexpensive down-market 'digs' and ate in cheap restaurants because that was about all we could afford.

Following my stint on the club circuit, my London agent booked me into the Royal Stratford Theatre, which is a turn-of-the-century classic theatre, to be the MC for a show called *Boys Will Be Girls,* leading me to think that things were starting to look up for my career. Little did I know that I'd be working two shows a night for two weeks with a cast of female impersonators. The performers with whom I shared the stage were funny, entertaining and although what they did was unusual to me, I have to say that they were also great company. However, just in case you are wondering, I did have my own dressing room, so I am no wiser than you as to the secrets of their trade.

Following that, the same agent booked me with two nightclubs in Leicester Square. They used to call this doubling, as the clubs were owned by two separate organizations. The first show was at 8:30 p.m. and the second at 11:30 p.m. As I recall, the first show went off without a hitch, which is quite something for an opening night. For the second show, however, I was escorted into the show lounge through the back door, while my wife had to enter the club through the front door. So there I am in the middle of my opening number when I see the maître d' escorting my wife to a table with four gentlemen. I quickly discovered that this was an escort club and he mistook her identity. I quickly stopped the music, and said "Hey, that lady is my wife and she sits with me."

On another booking at a nightclub in Barclay Square owned by the actor George Raft, I was told point blank, "Comics never make it here, only singers and dancers score with this crowd." At the time, I didn't comprehend how this could be. After all, they had to have an MC, no matter what kind of show they were putting on. But sure enough, with the house lights up and the comic doing his stuff, absolutely no one laughed. It turned out that this was another type of escort club and having the house lights on was simply bad for business.

Could it get any worse than this?

The answer is, "Yes, it could."

And it did.

Shortly after, I found myself booked on a series of gigs in the deepest, darkest corner of Wales, doing a circuit of 20 working men's clubs for six pounds a night, trying to get blokes who had been down in the mines all day to enjoy a few laughs with a beer.

Now, despite my father's heritage, I knew almost nothing about Wales. I couldn't pronounce the names of half the towns I was visiting and knew even less about the local custom and lore. "That doesn't really matter," I told myself. "After all, humour has universal appeal."

So it was on a rainy night in a small Welsh village, that after the singer and the magician, on came Peter. I took the stage and immediately went into my jokes about kids, which included hard-driving stories about how rotten they can be, how ungrateful and unnecessary they are and how, when they're in their early teens, their parents suddenly become stupid. This was really funny stuff that had cracked them up in London. On this night, there was not a single laugh. In fact, not even a murmur of a laugh.

Twelve minutes later, I gave up and walked off the stage, right into the arms of the furious club owner. "On your way, mate," he growled, without any further explanation of what I had done wrong. I wasn't about to ask any questions either. His clenched mouth and fierce eyes said it all, "GET OUT OF TOWN!"

Somewhat puzzled and upset at the lack of response I had received for what I knew was a positive routine, I drove out of town. As I did, I caught sight of a sign with the town's name on it and it finally clicked in my mind.

The town was Aberfan, and not a month before, from high on a slope above the town's small primary school, a monstrous pile of earth that was left over from the diggings in the coal mine had dislodged and slid down the hillside. It covered the school and surrounding buildings like a great grey blanket, taking the lives of 170 people, most of them children. It was the worst disaster of its kind in history and many of the working men in the club that night had been the fathers of those children, still filled with the memories of the faces and lives of those young Welsh citizens who had died beneath the Aberfan tip.

The realization hit me in the pit of my stomach and I felt

physically sick knowing that I had added to the grief of those bereaved fathers. It is a lesson I have never forgotten. If you are going to get up in front of people and open your mouth, it is so important to know where you are and to have some kind of knowledge about what's going on. And if you don't, you might get exactly what you deserve, just as I did that night in Aberfan.

The lessons kept mounting, but I never gave up. Something inside me said, "You must keep trying, don't give up, the best is yet to be."

The experience I was gaining was preparing me for a career I had not yet considered, and today I can tell you that everything counts along the way. I was, however, getting discouraged with my progress in the U.K. Despite the fact that I had my own television show on BBC TV, worked the Playboy Club on Park Lane (along with other clubs for U.S. servicemen in and around London), and even signed a contract to perform on the first Engelbert Humperdinck television show for ABC TV (it was to be filmed in Elstree Studios, starring Tom Jones, Jose Feliciano, Barbara Eden and myself), I was beginning to realize that show business wasn't as secure as I had hoped and I made the painful decision to return to Vancouver to pursue a career in business and more specifically, the media industry.

Upon my return to Vancouver, legendary impresario Ben Koplow booked me into the Cave theatre restaurant with the Mills Brothers. It was a wonderful welcome home and more than I thought I deserved. Although I continued to perform at the Cave from time to time with artists such as Damita Jo, Bobbie Gentry, OC Smith and on several more occasions, the Mills Brothers; I would soon discover that it was another career I was preparing for.

I got my first taste of that other career when I was invited to speak at a roast for Vancouver's Chief of Police at the time, Bob

Stewart. It was a Christmastime fundraiser and an enthusiastic audience filled the entire ballroom at the Hyatt hotel. I remember one of the roasters was a member of the Irish Rovers. The whole evening was a huge success and soon afterwards I had more invitations to emcee.

My speaking career, the one that I didn't know I was being trained for, had begun.

CHAPTER 2

*"It is very easy to overestimate
the importance of our own achievements in
comparison with what we owe others."*

— Dietrich Bonhoeffer

Masterpiece Tool:
Understand That No One Makes It Alone

It's been said many times that no one is successful unless someone else wants them to be. No one becomes successful all by themselves. Everything you want in life requires the support or cooperation of another individual.

A few years ago, I was speaking in Vienna, Austria, for the H.Y. Louie Company. As you may already know, Vienna is recognized around the world as a city that has both produced great masters and inspired great masterpieces. Among them are the symphonies of Wolfgang Amadeus Mozart, Ludwig van Beethoven, Joseph Haydn and Franz Schubert; the waltzes of Johann Strauss; the paintings of Gustav Klimt; Daniel Swarovski's inspired crystal works and Sigmund Freud's many theories regarding psychology and psychoanalysis.

On a tour of the city, my wife Kay and I discovered the Albertina Museum, which is directly behind the magnificent Vienna Opera House. While touring the museum, I discovered one of the most amazing stories about a work of art created by Albrecht Dürer that has influenced me over the years. Although the tale itself may not be strictly true, it still offers an invaluable and enduring lesson that I believe is worth sharing.

As the legend goes, Albrecht Dürer had a brother by the name of Albert and they both shared a dream to attend the University of Nuremberg to study art. However, coming from a very large family, they didn't want to ask their father to pay for their education, as they knew all too well he was struggling just to put food on the table for his growing family. So they decided to toss a coin and the winner of the coin toss would go to university and study art for four years. The loser would go to work in the salt mines in Vienna in order to earn sufficient money to put the other brother through school. As luck would have it, Albrecht Dürer won the coin toss, and Albert Dürer went to the salt mines.

After four years of study, Albrecht truly became a master-piece. He excelled in sketching and drawing, and his technique and skill overshadowed those of his professors. Upon graduation, the entire family had a celebratory dinner. Albert was at one end of the table, Albrecht, the other. About halfway through the meal, Albrecht stood up holding a glass of wine, looked directly at his brother and said, "I salute you, dear brother, and now it is your turn to go to the university and it is my turn to go to the salt mines."

Every head in the room turned toward Albert as he lifted his big, gnarled hands over his face to hide the tears that were streaming from his eyes. After a few moments, he looked back at his brother and said, "After four years in the salt mine, every finger in both of my hands has been smashed and broken so many times that I could never hold a chisel, a paintbrush, a palette or even a pen." And then he cried out, "It is too late for me! It is just too late for me."

Today, hanging on the wall of the Albertina Museum in Vienna is the original of Albrecht Dürer's most enduring drawing. It is a drawing that has been reproduced for museums and art galleries around the world and a copy of which also hangs in my own home in Canada. The piece is titled *Praying Hands* and the hands depicted are supposedly those of Albert Dürer, drawn by a brother who was so thankful for the enormous sacrifice that was made just so that he could become the master artist.

While this story may not have actually occurred in fact, the lesson it teaches us is still important. Most of us have someone who has sacrificed for us to become all that we are. As Oprah Winfrey once said, "The whole point of being alive is to evolve into the complete person you were intended to be."

Who has sacrificed to help you to be successful?

Is it a parent, brother, sister, aunt, uncle, boss, neighbour, your spouse, perhaps even your children? What have you done to acknowledge their sacrifice and thank them for making your success possible? Additionally, who has sacrificed for your organization to be successful and how have you rewarded them?

I'm sure if you are a business owner like myself, or even a manager, your staff have contributed greatly to the achievements that have been credited to your career. Throughout this book are some wonderful stories from members of the Canada Wide Magazines staff, who have all invested their time and energy to help me to be the best I can be. I thank them for their contribution to my success and also for their stories, which are a touching tribute to the values that have kept our company strong through 30 years.

A MASTER KNOWS: How important it is, each time you receive recognition for your accomplishments, to take the time to thank those who have helped to make you successful.

CHAPTER 3

"It's not your salary that makes you rich,
it's your spending habits."
— Charles A. Jaffe

Masterpiece Tool:
Expand Your Asset Base

According to Thomas J. Stanley, PhD, and author of *The Millionaire Mind*, you don't need a high IQ or an expensive business-school education to become a millionaire. While conducting research for his book, Dr. Stanley interviewed more than 1,300 millionaires in the U.S. to find out what common traits had contributed to their economic success.

Surprisingly, the typical millionaire did not inherit money from family, graduate from an Ivy League college or strike it rich with a stock play. In fact, Dr. Stanley points out that rather than choose a career strictly for the money, millionaires tend to choose careers that match their abilities and then they work harder than most people are willing to do to build up their asset base. They also tend to be practical (not prone to a lavish lifestyle) and willing to take calculated risks.

In his interviews, Dr. Stanley asked the millionaires which attributes they thought had contributed to their success. Here are their top four answers:

1. Ability to get along with people   61%

2. Possess strong leadership qualities   45%

3. Ability to sell my ideas/products   45%

4. Having good mentors   29%

How many of these attributes have you mastered in your own life?

Jim Rohn, who has been a mentor to many millionaires, says that the main reason to set a goal to become a millionaire is not for the money, but rather for what you become in the process of achieving the goal. It is sage advice that is echoed by Jack Canfield, co-author of *Chicken Soup for the Soul,* who, in Mike Litman's book *Conversations with Millionaires,* reveals, "I had to learn how to overcome my fears. I had to learn how to talk in front of groups. I had to learn how to plan a speech. I had to learn how to ask people I was initially afraid of to loan me money, etc. All of that was scary. But, when I did it and survived it, I was no longer afraid to do it in the future. Now you can take away my house, my money, my car and everything, and it wouldn't matter. I know how to create more of those things because of who I've become, NOT what I possess."

A MASTER KNOWS: When you want something, you have to be willing to pay your dues.

These lessons about mastering skills that can help to build your asset base also apply to growing a business. Over the years, Canada Wide Magazines has been approached many times by people or organizations that own a single publication. Because we are a larger company that has successfully diversified over the years, they come to us for advice on how to expand and grow their business. In most cases, the biggest problem they face is that in order to divert the cash flow necessary to launch a second title, they would have to put their current title in financial jeopardy.

As with many things in business, the solution to this problem is simple, but not easy. Knowing that the publishing business can be volatile and also realizing that while an individual publication may do well over the long term, it will likely not make its sales numbers each and every month of the year, Canada Wide has always maintained a retained earnings in excess of $1 million to ensure that we can support all of our publications. We have also never believed in carrying debt, not even to finance growth. As a result, I am proud to say that we have been able to grow to 36 titles and have lost very few contract publications over the years.

My advice to other companies is also simple, but not easy. First of all, in order to provide more stability over the long term, I recommend that growth be handled thoughtfully and carefully. It is important to have a plan. Our plan was to add one publication for each year of business. It is this kind of slow, steady growth that leads you to be an overnight success (or so people think) 30 years later.

In addition, all of the assets we have built at Canada Wide are directly related to publishing and the services needed for publishing. Rather than getting into selling something that we know nothing about, we've remained focused on our expertise.

Finally, we always think before we spend money. This is one of the places where many people fall down, when times are good they live high on the hog, not thinking that there may yet be leaner times ahead or the need to finance acquisitions that could greatly expand their business empire. By managing our operations prudently and diversifying to include value-added services such as graphic design, newsletter publishing and printing, we have managed to make the necessary capital available to invest when we've needed it.

———•••———

"You miss 100% of the shots you never take."

— Wayne Gretzky

———•••———

I took my friend and mentor, legendary Vancouver businessman Joe Segal, out to lunch for his 80th birthday and asked him what one thing he regretted not doing in his first 80 years. He answered, "I didn't risk enough." When he first said this, I shook my head in amazement, not understanding his answer. After all, here was a man who had accomplished great things in his life (very few individuals have started with less and built more than Joe) and attained great wealth (which he has used to help so many others).

"What more could he possibly want from life?" I puzzled to myself.

I soon realized from his explanation that Joe saw it differently.

"If I had risked more," he told me. "I could have been five times more successful that I am today and just imagine how much more I could have done for the community."

———•••———

They say that money talks and it's true; if we aren't mindful of how we manage it, it says, "goodbye." During the recent federal election in Canada, I was listening to CBC radio and heard a frightening statistic. A commentator was talking about the sustainability of our economy and noted that by the year 2015, this country will have more citizens over the age of 60 (of retirement age) than it will have people of working age. Given that a large number of these people are going to be dependent on the government for pensions, health care and even income assistance, it is just one more reason why, in the course of our career, we need to set a goal of retiring independently wealthy (i.e., having at least $1 million in personal assets).

And once you've accumulated your wealth, the best way to hold onto it, according to a new study, is to stay married. The study, which began in 1985 and involved 9,000 Americans who were between the ages of 21 and 28 at the time, concluded that staying married for life almost doubles your wealth. By tracking subjects over a 15-year period, assessing their stocks, shares, assets, bank accounts and properties, the study's author, Jay Zagorsky, came to the conclusion that married people ended up much wealthier than their single or divorced counterparts.

The study also found that married people accumulate wealth much faster than single people. Over the course of the study, single people accumulated a median of $1,500 at the beginning up to $10,900 in the 15th year. In the same period of time, married people gained 93 per cent more than their single or divorced counterparts.

Unfortunately, a lot of people don't understand the difference between income and wealth. Having a big salary doesn't mean you can afford to live an affluent lifestyle. Many people have learned this lesson the hard way when their comfortable, well-paid corporate positions disappeared and left them unable to maintain the expensive lifestyle to which they had become accustomed. Building wealth involves budgeting, saving, investing, controlling debt and setting clear financial goals.

—————

Here are some tips to help you work on increasing your asset base:
1. First off, check your attitude. How you approach the task of

financing your future will have an impact on the results you achieve. Rather than looking upon saving and investing as a burden on your disposable income, try telling yourself, "I am building my personal and family wealth."

2. Set measurable goals. Just as with every other area of your life, you will experience more success with your wealth-building strategy if you set both short and long-term goals to focus on. Short-term goals could include paying off any unnecessary debt you are carrying (such as credit card debt) personally or within your business. Long-term goals, focused on expansion and eventually retirement, should also have annual targets to keep you on track. It is important to set a realistic timeframe for each goal and then break the cost into manageable chunks based on your income and expenses.

3. Pay yourself. After you've taken care of your debts, start paying yourself and sock this money away in an emergency fund so you can avoid using credit cards to pay for unexpected expenses when they crop up. Once you've accumulated a cushion, you can put some of the money into an income-producing investment to get it working for you.

4. Make sure you are calculating your net worth accurately. Although you can list your luxury car, designer clothes and plasma screen TV on the plus side of your balance sheet, keep in mind that they are all depreciating assets and can distort what you think you have. Make sure that you are not spending more on these than you are putting into real estate, retirement funds or your savings account.

5. Train yourself to be a conscious consumer. Avoid robotically buying things you don't really need just because they're on sale. Also steer clear of unnecessary bank fees, like ATM charges and late-payment penalties, as well as credit cards with high interest rates and don't be shy about saving big bucks by negotiating the price down when buying a big-ticket item like a car.

6. Make a decision to be wealthy. The power of the mind, once it is made up and focused on a goal, is a powerful force. Unfortunately, most people never decide what they truly want in life; therefore they get little more than they expect. The process of deciding that you will be a success, have a great marriage, strong relationship with your children, or certain type of business or wealth will, in itself, cause you to move forward towards your goal. Your conscious decision will cause your mind to diligently search and create the reality that you have chosen.

7. Create a schedule that encompasses your whole life. To create balance in your life, you must factor in time for both your business and your personal life. I have seen far too many professionals sacrifice their family to achieve a goal only to find that when they finally reach it, they have no one to share their success with or they realize what little importance that goal had compared to the damage it did to their family.

Try using a "time block" system where you schedule specific time for each daily activity. The better you time block, the more effective you will be and the more that you adhere to the schedule, the more success you will have as a time manager. Remember to allow for a little "down time" or "flex time"; you'll need it to relax and decompress so you can stay focused and sharp during your "up time." Give yourself 15 minutes of flex time every two to three hours. This should be sufficient to de-stress or catch up so that you are able to stay focused and on schedule.

8. Define what the high-payoff activities are for you in your business and invest your time in these. Once you have determined these activities, you need the discipline to do them daily. These are the only activities you can do if you want to pay yourself well. The following are examples of high-payoff activities: prospecting, lead follow-up, client appointments, negotiating contracts, developing new products or services and business planning. You must focus, like an attorney does, on billing out hours daily. The more hours you bill, the more income you make. The greater percentage of the day spent on these activities, the more income earned.

9. Invest others with responsibility. In other words, learn to delegate! If you want to focus on the high-payoff activities, you need to teach and train your staff to replace you in certain functions. Keep in mind that they are bound to make mistakes as they learn; just as you made mistakes that turned into the valuable lessons that helped you develop your skills. Monitor their progress along the way and make sure you provide both constructive direction and praise for improvement.

10. Put good systems in place as soon as you possibly can. Luckily for me, I stumbled across this important lesson early on in my publishing career. Almost 29 years ago I went to a seminar at the Hilton Hotel in New York for an industry event called Folio that is expressly focused on the magazine industry. At the time, we only had the one magazine, *TV Week*, and I was completely overwhelmed by the size of the conference and the level of information available. Somehow, I stumbled into a breakout session on how to deal with the finances of a magazine. This would have been in the pre-PowerPoint days and the presenter had a slide on the screen that represented a typical financial statement. Pointing to the slide, he drew the delegates' attention to the numbers on the bottom of the statement and he asked us, "What are those numbers down there?"

"That's the bottom line," everyone responded in unison.

"That's correct," he said. "The first couple of lines on the top of your statement is your income followed by anywhere from 20 to

40 entry lines of expenses, which leaves you with the bottom line. You never want the bottom line to be in brackets, because that means you're losing money.

"I want to give you another term for the bottom line," he continued. "The bottom line is now called 'what's left' because there should always be something left over at the end of the month and at the end of the year.

"Now, I want you to take the number that is 'what's left' or 'the bottom line' and make it your 'top line,' meaning the most important thing that you pay attention to in your business. As an example, let's assume that 'Magazine X' can make $10,000 per issue. That becomes your top line. Then you work backwards, figuring out what your income and expenses will be in order to make your top line happen. You focus on your top line first."

I brought this lesson back with me from New York and immediately applied it to my own business. It's not very complicated or sophisticated, but it works and 30 years later, with 38 divisions of the company, it's the principle by which we manage each and every one of them. Does it work? In 30 years we have never, ever lost money — in comparison, the newspapers are littered with bankruptcy notices from all of the businesses on this continent whose management had not paid attention to or understood the numbers on a financial statement. We also give generously to the community, pay our staff well and have very nice offices . . . but we never, ever, lose sight of the top line.

CHAPTER 4

"What I do today is important because I am
exchanging a day of my life for it."

— Anonymous

Masterpiece Tool:
Make Every Moment Count

According to the human resources experts at Robert Half International, the average employee works only 50 per cent of the time they are at work. The other 50 per cent of their time is largely wasted on idle chit-chat with co-workers, late arrivals, extended coffee breaks and lunches, early departures, private phone calls and other personal business.

"Don't major in the minors," my dad always told me. "Do the tough things first and take control of both your career and your future."

It's good advice, and I would add the following, "Resolve to work all of the time that you are at work. If you are finding it difficult, try giving yourself a little reminder like 'back to work' each time that you realize you've gotten off track."

Contrary to what some experts will tell you, there is no magic formula when it comes to getting the hard work done or reaching your goals. If you wait around for inspiration to get you going, you might be waiting for a long time. A much more practical approach, and the one that has worked for me, is to methodically work towards your goal. If you want to know how effective what you are doing is, break it down into every action and ask yourself this question, "Will what I am doing right now take me toward my goals or away from them?"

———•———

A MASTER KNOWS: If you're not spending time working towards what you ultimately want to achieve, you're just wasting time.

———•———

Here is a story from Tracy McRitchie, Circulation Director for Canada Wide, about how she turned the opportunities at hand into something more.

My story of Canada Wide Magazines begins back on my 19th birthday, when I was a starving student at Simon Fraser University. I was celebrating at a bar with a new friend I had met at SFU and she brought her boyfriend at the time and his friend, Mark Weeks. Mark and I got along nicely, there were no fireworks between us — and as we ended up working together, that was all for the best — but it was definitely a cordial evening.

After a couple of cocktails the conversation moved on to work and what Mark did for a living — he was the Circulation Director at Canada Wide — and the fact that I was in desperately in need of funds. He mentioned that the company had recently acquired a new magazine called *BCBusiness* that needed some attention. I jumped at the chance and the following week began the job of sorting hundreds of magazines that had been returned by Canada Post into alphabetical order . . . boring!

I moved on from sorting cover returns to answering *TV Week* subscription phone calls, doing bank deposits and subscription data entry. When my workload at university increased, I cut back my duties at Canada Wide to the task of entering data for *TV Week*'s free subscriptions on the weekends with fellow staffer Trisha Soper. What fun we had, with our tunes blaring in the empty office, both of us typing at the speed of light to try to break our own records set the weekend before. I have great memories of those times.

Late in 1993, after I had finished the last of my exams and successfully completed my Bachelor of Business degree, I began to work full time with Mark in the circulation department in a new position that had been created to handle the increasing workload. Although it wasn't my dream come true, it was a full-time job that had literally fallen at my doorstep, so who was I to say no?

At that point in time, the circulation department was taking on a couple of large tasks. The first was moving both the *BCBusiness* and *Manitoba Business* magazine data files onto our current circulation software (previously the data handling for these publications had been outsourced to another company). The second large undertaking was the in-house printing of magazine labels for these two titles as well as the *Westworld* magazines. I tackled these new projects with Mark (we shared an office at the time so it was an intense learning environment for me) and I was surprised at the challenge but also at how much this work interested and intrigued me.

So many things have changed within the company since those days. We have added many more titles to our CWM family and created a direct-marketing department that coordinates numerous direct-mail campaigns for our clients. We also purchased and implemented much more sophisticated circulation software. My friend and teacher for 10 years, Mark Weeks, left the company after 18 years, and today, I am the Circulation Director.

"Well, you finally got my job!" Mark said when he called me to say congratulations.

During those 15 years, as we acquired and created new publications there were always new opportunities for me. I am proud to say that I have worked in every position in this department and in my current role as director, really appreciate the perspective that this experience has given me. When Mark first decided to leave the circulation department to become General Manager of *TV Week* magazine, Samantha Legge took over "temporarily" . . . for four years. She proved to be a strong and generous leader for our department. Sam taught me the other side of leadership, which is allowing people to learn and to grow. She also taught me how to delegate with confidence, and the importance of taking the time to learn about your staff and manage each person differently in order to satisfy who they are as individuals. Sam really boosted my confidence by allowing me to manage the department under her guidance, which really was the preparation I needed in order to tackle the role of director when the opportunity presented itself.

In all of the years that I have worked at Canada Wide, this company has never, ever held me back. I have had two children during that time and my goal while they are young is to spend as much time at home with them as I can. Canada Wide has allowed me to do this, supporting my decisions and allowing me the opportunity to grow in the company nonetheless. I am the first to realize that I am being allowed to have my cake and eat it too. I know this and am thankful each and every day for it.

I feel strongly that without working my way through this department and having such an incredible team of support (both within the department and throughout the company as a whole), I could never manage to do this job, which has led me to the realization that Canada Wide is proving to be a great place to spend all of my working years.

———•———

"Destiny is not a matter of chance. It is a matter of choice: it is not to be waited for, it is a thing to be achieved."
— William Jennings Bryan

———•———

Of course, making the most of every moment and every opportunity isn't just about the time we spend on our career. It also applies to our personal life and our relationships with those we love. In my own life, I have learned that sometimes you have to step outside the box of conventionality in order to make the most of the opportunities that life presents to you. That's exactly what I decided to do when my daughter announced that she was getting married.

Here's what happened.

In all the years that Canada Wide Magazines has been operating, we've always had more women on our staff than men. Needless to say, in that time there have been dozens and dozens of young women I have known who, in the lead-up to getting married, have had wedding showers thrown for them and yet, I can't ever remember being invited to one of them. It's virtually a women's only club and I'm really okay with that.

So it was that when my eldest daughter Samantha got engaged, my wife and some of Sam's close friends put on a number of showers for her. As best I can remember, I was probably reluctantly invited to them, but again I felt it was for women only. At the same time, I too wanted to do something with Sam to celebrate her upcoming marriage.

I thought about it for a long time before it suddenly dawned on me that I wasn't the only man who was being left out in the cold by this tradition. Because Samantha was working at Canada Wide Magazines, I happened to know that many of her associates in the advertising agencies, PR companies, television stations and hotels with which we did business were of the male persuasion.

I decided to throw my own wedding shower for Samantha and invite all of these men. I rented Dario's Italian Restaurant in Vancouver and put on a luncheon/shower for 100 male business associates of Sam's. Each guest was asked to bring one gift, a bottle of the vintage wine of their choice. The shower was a great success, Sam loved it and all the guys were thrilled to be invited to what may have been their first   and only   wedding shower.

A MASTER KNOWS: Things may come to those who wait, but only the things left by those who hustle.

Tamara Shewchuk, Production Coordinator for *BCBusiness*, shares her perspective on what it feels like to find a place where you belong.

Although I've been here at Canada Wide for just five months, after my first few frenetic weeks I couldn't imagine being anywhere else. It feels like home. Publishing has always been my first love, and after some years in the communications and public relations industry, an opportunity at Canada Wide came my way.

At first, I was hesitant to pursue the job as Production Coordinator. After all, I knew if I wanted to, I could go to work downtown in a big office with a stellar view or make more money with less stress and fewer deadlines, but two things pushed me to take the risk:

1. I had always had a dream to work "in magazines." Well, OK, to start my own magazine as a matter of fact, and;

2. While I had enjoyed my career so far, I had never felt truly passionate about any of the jobs I had done or the companies that I had worked for.

I went ahead and applied for the job. As I moved through the hiring process, I kept reminding myself from time to time that no one ever takes a risk they regret and that no matter what, the direction I should be taking in my life would present itself. Thankfully, it did, and I have no regrets. I think sometimes you don't know how wrong something has been, until you find what's right.

At Canada Wide, for the first time in my life, I am surrounded by people who share the same passion as me and are not working just for the money or the perks. It's great to go to work each day feeling excited about what I do. CWM feels like home because I know I am not alone and I know it's not just any company. The people here are valued as much as the profit they create, and there is a real opportunity to start at the bottom and rise to the top. Even being so new, I can see why so many people have been here as long as they have, with no intentions of going elsewhere.

The last five months have been amazing and I am looking forward to the day when I will receive my 10-year watch.

CHAPTER 5

*"Our deeds still travel with us from afar. And what
we have been makes us what we are."*
— George Eliot

Masterpiece Tool:
Following Through

In 2003, when I became chair of The Vancouver Board of Trade, the very first event that I was scheduled to host was a luncheon with guest speaker Darren Entwistle, President and CEO of the Canadian communications company, Telus.

On that day, we had a sellout crowd of 750 people at the Bayshore Hotel in downtown Vancouver. As chair, I was very excited and looking forward to the task. As such, I arrived at the hotel a bit early just as Darren was finishing his rehearsal and sound check. I introduced myself as he was making notes with a very handsome-looking pen. I happened to mention to Darren that I thought it was a great-looking pen and to my surprise he offered to give it to me as a gift after the speech.

The luncheon went very well with my introductions and Darren's speech. As I commented on the success of the program and thanked him for his presentation, I looked on with some disappointment as Darren casually put the pen back into his pocket. Obviously, he had forgotten that he had offered it to me and I didn't have the jam to say, "Hey Darren, you promised me that pen."

In the days that followed, I didn't see Darren at all as I carried on with the busy schedule that my new duties with The Board dictated. So I was quite surprised when a package arrived from his office with the following handwritten note inside:

Peter,
Here is the pen I promised you. Use it well and thank you for a great luncheon.
Sincerely,
Darren

He had also included a very nice fleece vest with his company's logo on it and I still have both the pen and the vest to this day. Now, that's great follow-through.

———————

A MASTER KNOWS: *The mark of a good leader is to remember what you have committed to and then to follow through, no matter what.*

———————

About 15 years ago, I bought *BCBusiness* magazine from the legendary business billionaire Jimmy Pattison. If you know anything of Jimmy, it is that he is famous for buying companies, but he very rarely sells any piece of his empire. However, the publishing industry was new to him and somewhere along the way, he decided to sell *BCBusiness*. It was a most fortuitous decision for Canada Wide Magazines to acquire this property, as it revolutionized our company and allowed us to enter the business market in British Columbia in a new and exciting way.

When we closed the deal, I shook hands with Jimmy and

promised that I would make *BCBusiness* the leading regional business magazine in all of Canada — one that he would be proud of — and I believe we have done that.

In the November 2005 issue, we ran a story on the 25 most powerful business leaders in our province, and as you might imagine, Jimmy came out in the No. 1 spot (just between you and me, he didn't have much competition for that spot). Our *BCBusiness* editor and art director decided to feature him on the cover of that issue. After the magazine was published, I had the cover framed and sent to Jimmy with a dozen copies of the magazine and my sincere thanks.

Now you can imagine how busy Jimmy is with 27,000 employees and almost $5 billion a year in business all around the world, so you might think the last thing he would have time for is to phone and personally thank me for the gift. However, that's exactly what he did. In fact, Jimmy attempted to phone me on five different occasions, on five different days, until he reached me personally to show his appreciation for putting him on the cover of a magazine he once owned and for sending him a beautifully framed memento. Jimmy's attention to detail and follow-through is legendary.

In all things, big or small, be known as a person who follows through. I learned this from my friend and mentor Mel Cooper, who is one of the best. He always responds quickly and it is a trait that I both appreciate and emulate in my own life.

Not long ago, I was at a reception at the Hotel Vancouver for a crowd of 500 people, and Jim Rogers, who is president of the Rogers Financial Group, caught my eye from across the room. From some distance, he called out, "Hey Peter, I don't have a copy of your latest book *The Runway of Life.*" Amidst all the din in the room, I said to him, "No problem, Jim, I'll get you a copy."

Then next day, I signed a copy and sent it to him with a little note. A week later, I got a note from him saying, "Now I know why you are so successful. We were yelling across a crowded room and anyone else would have forgotten to send the book, but you remembered."

I don't even do business with Jim's company, but you can bet that anytime my name comes up in conversation with him, he is going to tell people that Peter Legge is one guy who follows through.

As you may have noted from all three of the stories in this chapter, it isn't always the big things that make the biggest difference to the people we encounter in our life. A simple gesture, like acknowledging the extra effort that someone has gone to on your behalf, taking care of a small detail when you say you will, or going the extra mile to do someone a favour when they need it most, is all that is needed to make you someone whom others will credit with having great follow-through.

CHAPTER 6

"A mind that has been stretched will never return to its original dimension."

— Albert Einstein

Masterpiece Tool:
Feeding Your Mind

About three years ago, I had a stroke. I don't think there is such a thing as a mild stroke. At the time, I was speaking for the American Mental Health Association at the Bayshore Hotel. With about 20 minutes to go in my session, I couldn't remember my stories, I couldn't find my place in my speech, I felt hot, sweaty and disoriented. Worst of all, I had the sensation that I was falling off the stage.

Not knowing any better and not even imagining that there could be anything wrong with me, I simply chalked it up to a stuffy room and continued on with my talk. After I finished my presentation, I moved to the back of the room where I generally sell my books and again noticed that something was a bit odd when I couldn't sign my name properly. However, I brushed this off as a side effect of fatigue and carried on. What I didn't recognize then was that I was experiencing the classic symptoms of a stroke, which include: sudden weakness and numbness, difficulty speaking, vision problems and severe headache or dizziness.

I had three of these symptoms.

Before leaving the hotel that afternoon, I had a glass of wine with the client to talk about the session and then drove myself home, still not realizing that anything was wrong.

The next morning when it was time to get out of bed, I discovered that I had lost a considerable amount of control over my coordination and movement. By sheer force of will I managed to get out of bed, shower, shave and somehow drive myself to the office and make it to my chair. That's where I was when Heather Parker, Vice President of Canada Wide, walked in the door. She took one look at me and said, "There is something wrong with you. I think you need medical attention." Heather got me up out of my chair and took me to a nearby clinic where they quickly determined that I had had what, in medical terminology, is known as a transient, ischemic attack, otherwise called a stroke. I was absolutely shocked.

While there are no visible signs of it now, following my stroke, it took me more than an hour to walk one block with a cane while holding onto my wife's arm. Given that most doctors will agree that they can't do much about a stroke that you have just had (they can only help you to prevent a future stroke), I am absolutely thrilled at the recovery I have made. I was also happy to learn that a habit I have maintained for many, many years seems to have played a very positive role in that recovery.

It was about six weeks after my stroke that I went for a brain scan at the Royal Columbian Hospital in New Westminster. After the technician had completed the scan, he displayed the pictures of my brain on two computer screens and asked me if I would like to see them. Being more than a little curious, I said that I did and he proceeded to describe what was on the screens before me.

Although he knew that I was 60 years old, the technician didn't have any other information about me. So, after pointing out where my eyes, nose and ears were on the picture, in addition to the little Zorro-like "Z" where the stroke had left its mark, he turned and said to me, "If I didn't know you were 60, I would think that I am looking at the brain of a 40-year-old."

He then turned to my wife Kay and asked, "What does he do for a living?"

"He's in publishing," Kay replied.

"No, it's not that," he said.

"Well," said Kay, "He does perform a lot of community work."

"No, that wouldn't account for it either," he responded.

"He's also a professional speaker," Kay continued to provide ideas.

"No, it's not that either," The technician said, shaking his head. "He must do something else."

Kay then told him about how I have conditioned myself to read at least one book every week.

"Aha," he cried out. "That's it."

He asked how long I had been doing this and I told him, "Oh, about 20 years."

"That's definitely it!" the technician exclaimed, "Your habit of reading is what is keeping your brain young, and as long as you continue to exercise your mental capacity, your mind will remain agile."

"The only reason some people get lost in thought is because it's unfamiliar territory."

— Paul Fix

As I continued along the road to recovery, my doctor told me that whatever symptoms still remained six months after my stroke, I could expect to live with them for the rest of my life. Luckily for me, this wasn't to be the case. Although several symptoms persisted for as long as two years, today I feel that I am as good as I ever was, perhaps even better since the experience has led to a healthier and more balanced diet, regular exercise and a trimmer figure (30 pounds lighter and counting). I can't say that I always enjoy doing my exercise and watching what I eat, but I know that it's important and an investment in my health and longevity.

As a spokesperson for the Heart and Stroke Foundation of BC and the Yukon, I think it's important for people to understand that strokes don't just happen to other people and we all need to be aware of the warning signals. We also need to take responsibility for our lifestyle choices and do all we can to maintain our good health so we can achieve our masterpiece.

Continuing on with my 20-year habit, I continue to read a book a week. I think that it is just as important to keep your mind active and strong as it is your body. And we continue to have the capacity to learn just as long as we use it. Our brain only begins to age when we stop exercising it on a regular basis.

Personally, I like reading books on motivation, inspiration, business, leadership, biographies and autobiographies.

Famed speaker Earl Nightingale said, "If you read an hour a day on your chosen interest, you can be an international expert within seven years." And if you think you can't find the time to feed your mind, think again. If you're not an avid reader, try listening to tapes or attending seminars on topics that inspire you. Also, take the time to associate yourself with successful people whom you admire and find out what habits or traits helped them to achieve their success.

———•◦•———

A MASTER KNOWS: To read without reflecting is like eating without digesting.

———•••———

At the same time that you are feeding your mind with knowledge, you should also remember to eat whole foods that nourish your brain. Research shows that certain foods are high in nutrients that make your brain work better. These include:

B Vitamins — These play an important role in brain function. Vitamin B6 (pyridoxine) helps to convert tryptophan into serotonin and is found in chicken, pork, liver and kidney, fish, nuts and legumes. Thiamine, or vitamin B1, helps build and maintain healthy brain cells. You'll find thiamine in bread, rice, pasta and pork. Folic acid is also an essential "brain food" and is found in bananas, orange juice, strawberries, melons, lemons, green leafy vegetables, dried pulses and cereals.

Zinc — This mineral helps keep the senses sharp, as well as encouraging a healthy immune system. It is critical for proper growth and development in children. You'll find zinc in sunflower seeds, peanuts, red meat and oysters.

Omega-3 Fatty Acids — Found in fish like salmon and mackerel, Omega-3 can help stave off depression, a common side effect of stress. Research also reveals that Omega-3 is excellent for improving concentration and energy levels, and plays an important role in the reduction of heart disease and other ailments.

Fruit — As nutritionists will tell you, fresh fruit not only contains many of the vitamins and other nutrients needed for healthy brain function, but it also slowly releases natural sugars into the body and gives a sustained effect of mental and physical energy, unlike the "quick fix" that you get from consuming processed foods and sugary drinks.

Herbs — For many centuries, all kinds of herbs have been used by humans, not only for flavour in cooking but also as natural remedies. Try ginger to lift the spirits, basil to clear the mind, cinnamon to counteract exhaustion, chamomile (commonly found in tea) to help with nervous tension, and peppermint to help calm nerves and relieve anger.

———•—•———

To end this chapter on a light note, I hope you enjoy the following list of answers given by sixth-graders on their history tests. It was compiled and submitted to a web site for middle-school teachers.

1. Ancient Egypt was inhabited by mummies and they all wrote in hydraulics. They lived in the Sarah Dessert. The climate of the Sarah is such that the inhabitants have to live elsewhere.

2. Moses led the Hebrew slaves to the Red Sea, where they made unleavened bread, which is bread made without any ingredients. Moses went up on Mount Cyanide to get the Ten Commandments. He died before he ever reached Canada.

3. Solomom had three hundred wives and seven hundred porcupines.

4. The Greeks were a highly sculptured people, and without them we wouldn't have history. The Greeks also had myths. A myth is a female moth.

5. Socrates was a famous Greek teacher who went around giving people advice. They killed him. Socrates died from an overdose of wedlock. After his death, his career suffered a dramatic decline.

6. In the Olympic Games, Greeks ran races, jumped, hurled biscuits, and threw the java.

7. Julius Caesar extinguished himself on the battlefields of Gaul. The Ides of March murdered him because they thought he was

going to be made king. Dying, he gasped out: "Tee hee, Brutus."

8. Joan of Arc was burnt to a steak and was cannonized by Bernard Shaw.

9. It was an age of great inventions and discoveries. Gutenberg invented removable type and the Bible. Another important invention was the circulation of blood. Sir Walter Raleigh is a historical figure because he invented cigarettes and started smoking. Sir Fransis Drake circumsized the world with a 100-foot clipper.

10. The greatest writer of the Renaissance was William Shakespeare. He was born in the year 1564, supposedly on his birthday. He never made much money and is famous only because of his plays. He wrote tragedies, comedies, and hysterectomies, all in Islamic pentameter.

11. Writing at the same time as Shakespeare was Miguel Cervantes. He wrote Donkey Hote. The next great author was John Milton. Milton wrote *Paradise Lost*. Then his wife died and he wrote *Paradise Regained.*

12. Delegates from the original 13 states formed the Contented Congress. Thomas Jefferson, a Virgin, and Benjamin Franklin were two singers of the Declaration of Independence. Franklin discovered electricity by rubbing two cats backwards and declared, "A horse divided against itself cannot stand." Franklin died in 1790 and is still dead.

13. Abraham Lincoln became America's greatest Precedent. Lincoln's mother died in infancy, and he was born in a log cabin which he built with his own hands. Abraham Lincoln freed the slaves by signing the Emasculation Proclamation. On the night of April 14, 1865, Lincoln went to the theater and got shot in his seat by one of the actors in a moving picture show. They believe the assinator was John Wilkes Booth, a supposingly insane actor. This ruined Booth's career.

14. Johann Bach wrote a great many musical compositions and had a large number of children. In between he practiced on an old spinster which he kept up in his attic. Bach died from 1750 to the present. Bach was the most famous composer in the world and so was Handel. Handel was half German, half Italian and half English. He was very large.

15. Beethoven wrote music even though he was deaf. He was so deaf he wrote loud music. He took long walks in the forest even when everyone was calling for him. Beethoven expired in 1827 and later died for this.

CHAPTER 7

"Give me a firm place to stand and I will move the earth."

— Archimedes

Masterpiece Tool:
Goal Setting

My friend Joe Segal told me recently that "you either get bigger and better or you wither and die."

In terms of business, I believe that the "better" needs to come before the "bigger" to ensure that you have the right structures in place to manage growth when it happens, and the first important step to getting better at what you deliver is to set measurable goals with deadlines attached to them.

This also holds true for progress within your individual career. As a beginning public speaker, my first goal was to get as much experience under my belt as possible so that I could become a better speaker. To accomplish this goal, I offered to speak to groups and organizations for free. I did this for several years and as my skills improved, so too did my reputation as a speaker who could really connect with, and motivate, an audience. Not surprisingly, by this point my calendar was beginning to fill up with paid bookings and I was on my way.

Author and international speaker John Maxwell, who has produced some 40 books on leadership, once said, "Most people have no idea of how far they can go in life." This is one of the reasons why goals can be so helpful to us, because they move us forward one step at a time and before we know it, we have accomplished much more than we imagined we could.

My father once told me that most people "aim too low and succeed." If we hope to make a masterpiece of our life, what we need to focus on is aiming higher than we think we can reach.

As I have mentioned before, I have enjoyed the mentorship of Joe Segal for many, many years. We have lunch together about once a month and on both his 80th and 81st birthdays. As I mentioned earlier, Joe told me that one of his biggest regrets in life is that he didn't risk enough. I know that in saying this, Joe isn't talking about being irrational or foolish when making decisions and he isn't suggesting that he should have taken shortcuts (it's important to be able to look yourself in the mirror and know that you are a person of integrity). He is talking about pushing himself to do more with what he had.

The ability to step back to assess risk and consider the possible outcome of your decisions is an important skill that all masters must develop. Billionaire Jimmy Pattison once said, "You must do your homework on any kind of acquisition. Very often, the deal that I paid $1 for cost me the most."

Recently, Joe Segal was reflecting on my book *The Runway of Life* — which is based on his original concept that life is like a runway in that eventually you run out of tarmac, so you have to make something of yourself before it comes to an end. Anyway, Joe was musing about the numerous details a pilot has to take into account when they are preparing for takeoff — they need to make sure that the plane is fuelled and ready to go, there isn't any ice on the wings, the runway is clear and their instruments are functioning properly — in fact, the pilot has a whole list of details that he must check off before he takes to the air.

Now imagine what would happen if the pilot didn't bother with any of those details. What are the chances that the plane would manage to get off the ground successfully and if it did, that it would reach its destination safely; would you want to be on that flight?

How are you flying your plane?

Have you taken the time to actually define your goals, write them down and commit to them? If you haven't taken these three steps, then all you really have is a dream, not a goal and I am not just talking about career goals. I believe we need to plan for success in all aspects of our lives.

To help you review or set your own goals, here are some questions you might want to ask:

- Personal — How am I working to develop my character and become a role model for others?
- Spiritual — What are my most deeply held beliefs and what goals can I set to enrich and honour those beliefs?
- Health — What am I doing to ensure that my body and mind are strong? What personal habits can I replace to make myself healthier?
- Financial — How am I maximizing my financial resources to ensure that I can be self sufficient and take care of the needs of my family?
- Education — How am I taking advantage of opportunities to learn and grow? What am I doing to keep my mind active and expand my horizons?
- Career — How is the work that I am doing providing fulfillment in my own life and making a contribution to the world? Am I an asset to my organization and my profession? What can I focus on to move to the next level of achievement?

- Community — What am I contributing to my community to ensure that it is a place that I am proud to live in and pass on to my children? How can I mentor and support others so that they may develop their own talents?

———

Our goals become our master plan towards creating our masterpiece. One of the all-time best-selling books, Napoleon Hill's *Think & Grow Rich*, has sold millions and millions of copies. Hill once said, "You can't change where you started, but you can change the direction you are going."

That's what goals can do for you.

My good friend, speaker Brian Tracy, says that success in life results from goals, "Everything else is commentary." Whatever direction we are heading in life, it is a result of the goals that we have set. If you find that you're not going anywhere, chances are you don't have any goals to work towards; therefore you're just marking time.

Earl Nightingale, who is considered by many to be the dean of motivational speaking, often refers to a truth that is more than 2,000 years old. If you've ever listened to Earl speak or read his material, I'm sure you've heard him say, "You become what you think about most of the time." It is taken from King Solomon in Proverbs 22:30, who says, "As you think in your heart, so you shall be."

If you're thinking nothing — guess what? You get zip, nada, nothing, zero, diddly squat . . . well, you get the idea.

On the other hand, if you are thinking big, powerful positive thoughts and you back them up with sufficient knowledge and desire and sprinkle in a bit of calculated risk, it is truly amazing what you can accomplish.

Notice that we're talking about powerful "positive" thoughts. One of the difficulties we humans often encounter when we set out to accomplish something is fear and the negative thoughts that can result when we give in to our fear and conjure up all kinds of reasons why we won't be successful.

If you truly want to achieve your goals — and I believe you do, otherwise you wouldn't be wasting time reading this book — then you must consciously choose to stop focusing on what it is you fear. Each time a fearful or negative thought comes into your mind, replace it with a mental picture of your positive and worthwhile goal. You may find that making this shift in your thinking takes more effort than you imagined; that's because it's easier for a human being to think negatively than positively. That's why so few people actually accomplish their goals.

Another simple and very powerful thing you can do towards achieving your goals is to write them down. Fewer than three per cent of people have written down the goals they want to focus on. And yet, the mere act of committing your goals to paper increases the likelihood of achieving those goals by a whopping 100 per cent, that's just by writing them down. Take some time and write down your top 10 to 15 goals and make sure that you put them in the first person.

If you've done it, congratulations! You're now in the top three per cent.

To get into the top two per cent, write about your goals as if you have already achieved them. The reason for doing this is that something happens to the subconscious when you frame your goals this way. For example, achieving a healthy weight is a common goal that many people have. You would write the goal this way:

"I am maintaining a healthy weight of 150 pounds." Then do

whatever it takes to achieve that goal in a specific timeframe.

Not long ago, I set about getting my own weight under control and decided on a goal to lose 30 pounds within a two-year period. Not only am I happy to report that my goal was pretty much accomplished on time, it also resulted in the best blood pressure level I've had in 10 years. Today, I have more energy and feel so much better about myself knowing that it is within my control to take care of my physical well-being.

———

Now that you've defined your goals and written them down, how do you get into the top one per cent with those people who are most successful in life?

Simply write down your goals every morning before you leave the house to start your day in the world.

Why is this so important?

Well, do you remember the quote just a few paragraphs back that said, "You become what you think about most of the time"? I happen to be living proof that it is true. With that being the case, what do you want to focus your attention on?

Dr. Benjamin E. Mays, the late president of Morehouse College near Atlanta, wrote the following favourite passage of mine:

It must be borne in mind
That the tragedy in life
Does not lie in not reaching your goal,
The tragedy lies in having no goal to reach.
It is not a calamity to die with dreams unfulfilled,
But it is a calamity to have no dream.
It is not a disaster to be unable to capture your ideal,
But it is a disaster to have no ideal to capture.
It is not a disgrace not to reach the stars,

But it is a disgrace to have no stars to reach for.
Not failure, but low aim is sin.

———•·•———

A MASTER KNOWS: *If you haven't written it down, you haven't thought it through.*

———•·•———

Having goals is also a good way to stay focused when unexpected events happen in your life. Consider this story from Suzy Williamson, Production Manager with Canada Wide.

On a Wednesday we were told that our magazine was shutting its doors. By Friday, I was offered a position at Canada Wide. Still in shock over losing my job, I was unsure what I should do, travel the world? Bum around for a while and "find myself"? With four years in publishing under my belt, my career was still in its infancy so I did the sensible thing and accepted the Production Coordinator position at Canada Wide.

I was apprehensive at first, knowing little about my new employer, but 15 years later I feel like part of the furniture.

The hectic pace of magazine production and print management is difficult to describe. It's a bit like a roller-coaster ride, or like running a race where you must always be several months ahead of everyone else. The details and deadlines never cease. Let a ball drop and things fall apart.

There have been times when family or friends have wondered what keeps me in a job that requires such a constant high level of dedication, commitment and energy. I have to say that I love both the challenges and the constant learning, but most importantly, it's the amazing people I work with that keep me sane. I love the crazy pace and the collaboration with so many creative and intelligent people who love what they are doing too.

People at Canada Wide show a passion for their work that I don't often see in other workplaces. We all take pride in the wonderful end results, when compelling stories and excellent design come together on the printed page. I'm a magazine-lover at heart, and seeing our stable of publications grow and improve over the years makes me proud of our accomplishments.

Along with all of the hard work, there is also a huge "fun factor" at Canada Wide. Over the years I've joined staff in many company events, from themed potluck luncheons to baby showers, from golf tournaments to karaoke contests. There have also been many events to raise money for charitable organizations, something that has solidified Canada Wide's reputation as a generous corporate citizen.

I feel blessed to have developed lasting and precious friendships during my years with this company and I appreciate the challenges and opportunities that have allowed me to grow both personally and professionally.

———•·•———

Goal-setting should be a regular part of your overall planning, as should time for breaks that allow you to recharge and review both your goals and your progress towards them. Plan breaks in advance. If you plan time away, you will easily be able to get away without having to reschedule, juggle, cancel, delegate or rush to get things done. Take a stand for yourself and make sure that you get those needed breaks.

Another positive side effect of setting goals and other types of planning is that it can drastically reduce the amount of worry and stress in your life because it helps you to focus your attention and energy towards the things that you can and want to change.

———·•·———

Here is an inspiring story from one of Canada Wide's talented art directors, Anya Lewis, and how she pursued a goal and landed her dream job.

By the time I'd started university, I knew that when I "grew up" I wanted to work in the publishing business. More specifically, I wanted to design magazines. Therefore, upon arriving in Vancouver from Ontario, I had one goal in mind, to work as an art director for Canada Wide Magazines. From my research, I knew that Canada Wide was the biggest publisher in Western Canada, and my philosophy was, "Go big or go home!"

My only challenge was to find a way in. Then one day, I spotted an ad in the careers section of the newspaper. Canada Wide Magazines was looking for an art director for *TV Week*. I knew what I had to do. I was going to get that job.

I started by sending my résumé to VP of Production, Corinne Smith, just like the ad said to do. But what next, sit around and wait for the phone to ring? Not good enough. I needed to do something more, something to show her just how much I wanted that job.

A few days passed and I was still waiting for the phone to ring when a co-worker told me about an invitation she had to attend an awards dinner that night. When she told me it was the Western Magazine Awards gala, a light went on in my head. I absolutely had to be at that awards dinner to meet Corinne Smith. Luckily for me, my co-worker asked if I wanted to go and I readily accepted. I rushed home from work that afternoon to put together a great big package for Corinne; in it was my résumé and samples of my design work. I was excited, and nervous. I didn't know who

Corinne was or even what she looked like, but hopefully I'd get lucky and people would be wearing nametags so that I could pick her out. In any case, it didn't matter. Once I got to the reception I'd figure it out.

When we arrived at the reception, the room was very crowded with people, many of them without nametags. It took my co-worker and me a few minutes to find the person who had so kindly invited us. When we did, we exchanged hellos and then, to my utter amazement, she turned around and introduced us to Corinne Smith and art director Cathy Mullaly of Canada Wide.

Jackpot! I couldn't believe my luck until our contact introduced me and Corinne shook my hand and thanked me for my résumé, right in front of my co-worker. I was caught off guard, surprised that she remembered my name and concerned that my co-worker might spill the beans to my employer that I was in the market for a new job. I had to think fast, so I interrupted Corinne and said, "Wow, I'm really flattered that you remember my name, that was a few years ago now." Thankfully, she looked at me as if she knew exactly what I was trying to tell her and dropped the subject.

Eventually we sat down to dinner. I barely touched my food but I made sure that I could see Corinne from where I sat. I still had my résumé package tucked in my purse, looking for an opportunity to get it to her without being too obvious. Nervously, I waited for her to get up to use the ladies' room, or at least leave the room so I could follow her. Finally she did, and I was on her tail the minute she got up.

"Excuse me, Corinne," I said, my voice cracking with nervousness. I felt flushed and out of breath. "Excuse me, hi, um, I have something for you . . . and if this is completely inappropriate, please tell me."

"No," she said. "What is it?"

"I have a package here with my résumé in it and some samples of my work. Can I leave it with you and when you have a minute you could take a look at it?" I asked. "I've already emailed you a résumé for the job of art director, but I thought since you were here, this would give me a chance to introduce myself and at least let you see some samples of my work."

"Yes, of course, I got your email. Leave it with me," she said. "But you know, we're pretty late into our search, so I can't promise anything."

I don't remember much of the rest of that evening. I was over the moon at the possibility of landing my dream job.

I got a phone call the next day to come in for an interview and a week later I found out that the job was mine. The rest, as they say, is history. It just goes to show that you can achieve anything as long as you put your mind to it.

CHAPTER 8

*"Make everything as simple as possible,
but not simpler."*
— Albert Einstein

Masterpiece Tool:
Keep Things Simple

"Pluralitas non est ponenda sine necessitate," or in English,
"Plurality should not be posited without necessity." The words are
those of the medieval English philosopher and Franciscan monk
William of Ockham (ca. 1285-1349) who, as mentioned in Chapter
1, employed a method of problem-solving that has come to be
referred to as Ockham's Razor. At the heart of the method is the
idea that the simplest and most direct solution (requiring the fewest
number of steps) is usually the correct solution to any problem.

What Ockham realized is that the more complicated something
is (even if it is a good idea), the less likely it is to be implemented.
Therefore, if you have a problem and are torn between two
different solutions that in all likelihood will be equally effective if
fully implemented, then by applying Ockham's Razor, you will
naturally choose the solution that is less complicated. My own
interpretation of Ockham's Razor is, if you want to be a success in
life, don't overcomplicate either your goals or your problems.

"Great leaders are almost always great simplifiers, who can cut through argument, debate and doubt, to offer a solution everybody can understand."

— Colin Powell

Simplicity applies in so many areas:

Sometimes, all you need to survive in a competitive market is to do whatever the competition isn't doing. For example, some number of years ago when Domino's Pizza was expanding their franchise very quickly, they opened a location in a small community where their presence would most likely put a smaller local company out of business. However, this small operator wasn't going to take it lying down. He turned around and ran a campaign telling customers to bring him the Domino's ad out of the Yellow Pages and he would give them a 50 per cent discount on a pizza purchase from his restaurant.

As it turned out, this was a simple but very smart move on his part. For not only was he giving customers a good deal (something that all customers appreciate), he was also engaging customers in removing his major competitor's advertisement from their homes. In doing so, he demonstrated a resourcefulness that is vital to success as an entrepreneur. Rather than complaining, he took matters into his own hands and turned the situation to his advantage.

A MASTER KNOWS: In creating a statue, a sculptor doesn't add material on to his subject. Instead, he keeps chiseling away at the inessentials until the truth of his creation is revealed.

By selling safety, not tires, the people at Michelin are a good example of simplicity. They focus first on the needs of their customers rather than their own desire to sell more product and make more profit. In the end, they do sell more product because customers trust the company to take care of their needs.

Not paying attention to what customers wanted or needed was the ultimate downfall of the infamous PacifiCat Ferries. You might recall that these were three fancy passenger ferries the government of British Columbia paid $454 million to have built in the late 1990s. What the government forgot when they put the ferries into service was that they were in the economical transportation business. Instead, they thought they were in the high-speed, luxury-cruise business. What their customers wanted was very simply a reliable, safe and economical way to travel between the Lower Mainland and Vancouver Island — what they got were three big clumsy white elephants — for not only were the PacifiCats horribly expensive, but they were also too fast for their own good (causing up to 2.5-metre waves to crash onto the inhabited shorelines throughout Howe Sound).

After operating for little more than a year, the trio of aluminum-hulled ferries (one of which was never even used) were taken out of service and then sold at auction to the Washington Marine Group in March 2003 for just $20 million. The irony in this story is that WMG is thinking about bringing the ferries back into service on a Vancouver-to-Nanaimo route.

The PacifiCat Ferries fiasco was a major contributing factor in the downfall of that particular provincial government not long afterward, and it's a good reminder to all of us (in business and our relationships) that we should make sure we know what someone really wants or needs from us, before we decide to go ahead and give it to them.

This next story is an amusing example of what can happen when a simple request goes awry. It is an exchange that took place between a London hotel and one of their guests who was having a problem with soap. The story appeared in the *Sunday Times* of London.

Dear Maid,
Please do not leave any more of those little bars of soap in my bathroom since I have brought my own bath-size Dial. Please remove the six unopened little bars from the shelf under the medicine chest and another three in the shower soap dish. They are in my way.
Thank you,
S. Berman

Dear Room 635,
I am not your regular maid. She will be back tomorrow, Thursday, from her day off. I took the three hotel soaps out of the shower soap dish as you requested. The six bars on your shelf I took out of your way and put on top of your Kleenex dispenser in case you should change your mind. This leaves only the three bars I left today which my instructions from the management is to leave three soaps daily.
I hope this is satisfactory.
Kathy, Relief Maid

Dear Maid — I hope you are my regular maid.
Apparently Kathy did not tell you about my note to her concerning the little bars of soap. When I got back to my room this evening I found you had added three little Camays to the shelf under my medicine cabinet.

I am going to be here in the hotel for two weeks and have brought my own bath-size Dial so I won't need those six little Camays which are on the shelf. They are in my way when shaving, brushing teeth, etc.

Please remove them.

S. Berman

Dear Mr. Berman,

My day off was last Wed. so the relief maid left three hotel soaps which we are instructed by the management. I took the six soaps which were in your way on the shelf and put them in the soap dish where your Dial was. I put the Dial in the medicine cabinet for your convenience.

I didn't remove the three complimentary soaps which are always placed inside the medicine cabinet for all new check-ins and which you did not object to when you checked in last Monday. Please let me know if I can be of further assistance.

Your regular maid,

Dotty

Dear Mr. Berman,

The assistant manager, Mr. Kensedder, informed me this a.m. that you called him last evening and said you were unhappy with your maid service. I have assigned a new girl to your room. I hope you will accept my apologies for any past inconvenience. If you have any future complaints, please contact me so I can give it my personal attention. Call extension 1108 between 8 a.m. and 5 p.m. Thank you.

Elaine Carmen

Housekeeper

Dear Miss Carmen,

It is impossible to contact you by phone since I leave the hotel for business at 7:45 a.m. and don't get back before 5:30 or 6 p.m. That's the reason I called Mr. Kensedder last night. You were already off duty.

I only asked Mr. Kensedder if he could do anything about those little bars of soap. The new maid you assigned to me must have thought I was a new check-in today, since she left another three bars of hotel soap in my medicine cabinet along with her regular delivery of three bars on the bathroom shelf. In just five days here I have accumulated 24 little bars of soap. Why are you doing this to me?

S. Berman

Dear Mr. Berman

Your maid, Kathy, has been instructed to stop delivering soap to your room and remove the extra soaps. If I can be of further assistance, please call extension 1108 between 8 a.m. and 5 p.m.

Thank you,

Elaine Carmen

Housekeeper

Dear Mr. Kensedder,

My bath-size Dial is missing. Every bar of soap was taken from my room including my own bath-size Dial. I came in late last night and had to call the bellhop to bring me four little Cashmere Bouquets.

S. Berman

Dear Mr. Berman,

I have informed our housekeeper, Elaine Carmen, of your soap problem. I cannot understand why there was no soap in your room since our maids are instructed to leave three bars of soap each time they service a room. The situation will be rectified immediately. Please accept my apologies for the inconvenience.

Martin L. Kensedder

Assistant Manager

Dear Miss Carmen,

Who the hell left 54 little bars of Camay in my room? I came in last night and found 54 little bars of soap. I don't want 54 little bars of Camay. I want my one damn bar of bath-size Dial. Do you realize I have 54 bars of soap in here? All I want is my bath-size Dial.

Please give me back my bath-size Dial.

S. Berman

Dear Mr. Berman,

You complained of too much soap in your room so I had them removed.

Then you complained to Mr. Kensedder that all your soap was missing so I personally returned them. The 24 Camays which had been taken and the three Camays you are supposed to receive daily. I don't know anything about the four Cashmere Bouquets. Obviously your maid, Kathy, did not know I had returned your soaps so she also brought 24 Camays plus the three daily Camays. I don't know where you got the idea this hotel issues bath-size Dial. I was able to locate some bath-size Ivory which I left in your room.

Elaine Carmen

Housekeeper

Dear Miss Carmen,

Just a short note to bring you up-to-date on my latest soap inventory. As of today I possess: On shelf under medicine cabinet — 18

Camay in four stacks of four and one stack of two. On Kleenex dispenser — 11 Camay in two stacks of four and one stack of three. On bedroom dresser — one stack of three Cashmere Bouquet, one stack of four hotel-size Ivory, and eight Camay in two stacks of four. Inside medicine cabinet — 14 Camay in three stacks of four and one stack of two. In shower soap dish — six Camay, very moist. On northeast corner of tub — one Cashmere Bouquet, slightly used. On northwest corner of tub — six Camays in two stacks of three.

Please ask Kathy when she services my room to make sure the stacks are neatly piled and dusted. Also, please advise her that stacks of more than four have a tendency to tip. May I suggest that my bedroom window sill is not in use and will make an excellent spot for future soap deliveries.

One more item: I have purchased another bar of bath-size Dial which I am keeping in the hotel vault in order to avoid further misunderstandings.

S. Berman

CHAPTER 9

*"I could never have done what I have
done without the habits of punctuality, order and
diligence; without the determination to
concentrate myself on one subject at a time."*
— Charles Dickens

Masterpiece Tool:
Punctuality

How you do anything is how you do everything — if you have a clean car, a tidy office and an organized home, it reflects on your approach to business. Whether you like it or not, people will judge you by your habits. If you are late, the message it gives to others is: I'm more important than you.

Fewer than five per cent of people are punctual every single time; that's what makes them really stand out from everyone else. They are admired and respected by others. They are also considered to be more competent and valuable as a result of being punctual.

B.C. billionaire Jimmy Pattison is one such individual in both his business and his personal life. If you've been invited aboard Jimmy's boat, don't show up five minutes late because you'll be waving to the boat from the shore. If Jimmy says the boat leaves at 7 p.m., you can be darn sure that it will. This is a lesson that more than one person I know has learned the hard way.

I recently read a news story from Germany about another punctual fellow. The story made it into the papers because this guy had just won $27 million in the lottery. Apparently, he was on his way to work one morning when he stopped in at a corner store to buy his weekly lotto ticket and in checking his numbers from the previous week, the clerk informed him that he had won the jackpot.

The man's reaction to the news of his win left the lottery operator dumbfounded, according to the article.

"After he was told that he had won the jackpot, he said he didn't have time to chat because he would get into trouble with his boss if he was late to work," said the store clerk.

I think you have to admire someone who gets to work on time under those circumstances.

What Punctuality Says About You

1. *First and foremost, punctuality shows others that you care.* By keeping our commitments to others, we are acknowledging their needs. As business people, we should be concerned about caring for our customers since it is through our relationships that we build our business.

2. *Punctuality shows that you are confident.* When you show up on time, it is a sign that you are ready to take on whatever task or project lies before you. On the other hand, being late can imply that you lack confidence or that you are hesitant to deal with a person or situation, possibly because you don't have the skills, knowledge or tools to create a successful outcome. Confidence is the companion of success.

3. *Punctuality shows that you're in control.* Not only is it true that people want to do business with those they know, like

and trust; they also want to do business with people who are in control. Individuals who always arrive on time to appointments give the impression that they manage things well and are more likely to be reliable in everything they do.

4. *Punctuality shows that you hold yourself to high standards.* Just like honesty and integrity, punctuality is a standard for operating excellence. Not only does it imply that you are in control of your business, it also shows that you respect yourself and others. Successful, well-respected business people typically have punctuality as one of their highest values.

5. *Punctuality shows that you know how to keep things on track.* When you show up on time (or deliver your products and services on time), you keep your business moving forward. In doing so, you show that you understand that other people and events are also affected by what you do — or don't do. If you don't deliver as promised, you can negatively affect the plans of others. By showing up on time, you allow other people and things to show up on time as well, so that everybody benefits.

A MASTER KNOWS: If you improve the quality of your time management, you improve the quality of your life.

Read about time management on a regular basis. If you practice them diligently, personal time management habits will become automatic to you over time.

Here are some master habits to live by:
- Plan each day in advance.

- Resolve to be punctual for every appointment.
- Organize your daily work by priority.
- Overcome procrastination with planning.
- Prepare thoroughly for every important meeting (if it isn't worth preparing for, you are probably wasting your time by having a meeting at all).

CHAPTER 10

"Be your name Buxbaum or Bixby or Bray
or Mordecai Ali Van Allen O'Shea,
you're off to great places! Today is your day!
Your mountain is waiting — So . . .
get on your way!"

— Dr. Seuss

Masterpiece Tool:
Move Quickly on Opportunity

There's a story I like to tell about a painfully shy man who fell in love with a young woman. He sensed that she felt the same way, but he couldn't find the courage to ask her out. Finally, he decided he would mail her a love letter every day for one year and then ask her on a date. Faithfully, he followed his plan and at year's end he was courageous enough to call her — only to discover that she'd married the letter carrier.

If there is something you want to accomplish, do it now! Do it today! If there is something that you have been meaning to do or something you've been putting off, waiting for the perfect time to do it — do it today.

Today is that time. Today is the day to go ahead and get started. Right now is the time to make that first step. Don't wait any longer. If you intend to do it, prove it with your actions today. Go beyond thinking about it.

When I had a stroke a few years ago, I suddenly realized that I just don't know what the future holds and I can't take the chance that my body will be healthy and strong and capable forever. That's why I don't put off anything important that I want to accomplish . . . and you shouldn't either.

In the business world (as in the natural world), the market (or Mother Nature) favours those who can move quickly to take advantage of opportunity. That's why, as the saying goes, the early adapter (or bird) gets the customer (or the worm, as the case may be).

When it comes to satisfying the individual needs of customers, entrepreneurs have one very distinct advantage over larger companies, yet it is an advantage that often gets overlooked in the rush to be competitive on price or selection. It is the advantage of speed.

Due to their sheer size and bureaucracy, most large companies are slow to respond to changes in the market or to adjust products or services to meet the individual needs of the customer. As a business owner, the faster you can find out what your customers want and then provide it to them, the more attractive and valuable they will consider you.

A MASTER KNOWS: Enterprising people are those people disciplined and dedicated enough to seize opportunities that present themselves, regardless of the current situation, struggles, or obstacles.

Angela Bullock, an Account Manager for *TV Week*, tells how she seized the opportunity to move into a whole new career.

My career with Canada Wide Magazines began at Bimini's Restaurant over a drink with *TV Week* Retail Sales Manager

Jacquie Rogers and Canada Wide Marketing Manager Brianne Roe, both of whom play on an Ultimate frisbee team with me. One afternoon I happened to mention in conversation that I was ready for a challenge and really wanted to get into sales. "*TV Week* is looking for a sales rep," said Jacquie. "I think you should apply, you'd be perfect."

Although I was happily employed by the hotel, Delta Vancouver Suites, I really had wanted to get into sales for a long time. The only thing that was holding me back was my lack of direct selling experience. I wondered if they would consider giving me a chance despite that fact.

Later in the week, I received an email from Jacquie, stating that she really was serious about my applying and she had even mentioned it to her VP of Sales, Debbie McLean, who wanted me to come in for an interview as soon as possible.

"Don't worry if you don't have your résumé ready," she told me. "Debbie remembers dealing with you when you were working as a marketing and sales assistant at the Delta Whistler Village Suites." It was an extremely tough decision to consider leaving such a great company (I had been with Delta Hotels for the last five years). If I did leave, it would have to be for a top-quality company where employees are encouraged to contribute, grow and most importantly, have fun at work.

Thankfully, all of these elements were obvious during my interview with *TV Week* GM Mark Weeks, Debbie and Jacquie. Sitting at the boardroom table with these three professionals who together had invested more than 40 years into Canada Wide Magazines, I was impressed that they still had so much energy and enthusiasm for their workplace. This was definitely a company I wanted to be a part of. Needless to say, it's been eight months and not only have I surpassed my expectations by meeting and exceeding my sales budgets for the last five consecutive months, I also enjoy coming in to work every day. This was the best career decision I've ever made.

———•———

Here's another story about one of our team members, Senior Account Executive Bruce Jones, who knew a good thing when he saw it.

I had just parted ways with my employer in Vancouver and decided that it was time to return to my beloved Montreal. As I recall, it was midway through summer and my wife too was in between positions so we were ready to go. The only thing left to do was make the call to the moving company.

That is, until a chap that I had befriended at my local place of leisure slid onto his perch next to me at the bar and calmly said, "Hey Jones, my wife just left her job at Canada Wide Magazines and you could probably take her place there and make a few dollars to help pay for your move back to Montreal. That way you could make some cash and still leave in September."

That sounds perfect, I thought.

I joined Canada Wide in July of 1996 with the idea, as I mentioned, of leaving that September. It's been almost 10 years now . . . and I think I'll stay around awhile since it appears that I may have passed the probation period.

CHAPTER 11

*"People are lonely because they build
walls instead of bridges."*

— Joseph F. Newton

Masterpiece Tool:
Take Time to Build Your Relationships
with Others

Courtesy, in our everyday dealings with other people, is such a small thing and yet it can make all of the difference in the world. A favourite story of mine, which I've told in a previous book, took place a few years ago when I was in Las Vegas for a speaking engagement with Jaguar Canada. I had been staying at the Mirage Hotel and I had to leave early in the morning to catch my flight. I came down to the lobby at about 5:30 a.m. to check out and the young man at the front desk must have just been finishing up a night shift.

As I approached the counter, he asked me in a perfunctory way, "How are you this morning?"

"Just fantastic, thank you," I responded enthusiastically with a smile on my face.

The young fellow looked back at me with a sour expression and said, "And what makes you so fantastic this morning?"

"You know, young man, 3,200 60-year-old men didn't wake

up this morning," I said. "They're dead."

A shocked look came over the young man's face and then he looked me right in the eye and said, "I'm starting to feel better already."

———•—•———

Here is a story from Canada Wide's Senior Art Director, Rick Thibert, on a gesture that made a real difference for him and his family during a difficult time.

In 1990 I was between jobs and had taken on a position as a freelancer at Canada Wide Magazines in the production department to assist Corinne Smith, who is now the VP of Production. At the time, Corinne was the art director for *BCBusiness*, *Alberta Business* and *Manitoba Business* magazines.

Not long afterwards, I was offered a full-time position at Canada Wide, which I quickly accepted. From the start, the one thing I really noticed was that the company was like one big family, which was something I had not experienced at any other company I had previously worked for.

But it isn't just the great people and the wonderful working atmosphere that has kept me here at Canada Wide. Eight years ago, I fell ill with a very serious condition that required major surgery. Needless to say, I was devastated and very worried about everything, including my job, my family and my life!

Almost immediately after I received the diagnosis, Corinne came to me (and I know she spoke for the company) and said, "I want you to go home, get well and not worry about a thing. Your job at Canada Wide will be here waiting for you when you get back."

After a six-month recovery, I did go back to work and my job was indeed waiting for me. I cannot tell you how much this has meant to me and my family. Although I had considered Canada Wide as just a short footnote in my career when I started, I have now been here for 16 years and counting. I would like to take this opportunity to say thank you, Peter, for giving us a company to work for that allows us to grow and excel at our craft and truly supports us along the way.

I was browsing the Internet recently when I came across a blog site where a group of people had been discussing the topic of courtesy in modern times and one of them provided the following definition of courtesy, which I quite liked: *"Courtesy is the ability to acknowledge in a friendly way the human dignity of those around you, whatever the circumstances."*

Courtesy is so important to me and how my company does business that the last thing I do before I hire a senior-level person is to take them out for lunch to observe their manners and how they treat the restaurant staff throughout the meal. Apparently, I'm not the only one who does this. In fact, the *Vancouver Sun* newspaper recently ran a story on this very issue.

Here are some questions to help you check your courtesy quotient:

- Do you return phone calls and emails in a timely manner?
- Do you regularly express gratitude to those around you, especially when someone has done something nice for you?
- Are you available to others without making them feel like they're imposing?
- Do you make sure never to keep people waiting for longer than a few minutes to meet with you?
- Have you trained your staff to respond with courtesy and

politeness in all situations?

- Do you regularly ask others for input, and genuinely consider what they have offered?
- Do you notice when people are approaching a building at the same time as you and hold the door open for them?
- Are you generous with compliments and express them when others have done a good job?
- Do you always say please and thank you at restaurants, when you shop, when someone has helped you in some way?
- Do you allow the person with one grocery item to go ahead of you at the check-out?
- Do you allow other vehicles to move into the lane in front of you without honking your horn at them?
- Do you pay your bills on time, or let your creditors know if you cannot?
- Are you cautious about how you speak about others so as not to start rumours or spread gossip?
- Do you make sure never to put down your competitors or speak ill of them?
- Do your customers know that you value them, from your words and your deeds?
- Do you make every effort to curb your tongue when you feel like flying off the handle?

While all of these niceties may seem like small things — it really is the small gestures that we make towards others that leave a lasting impression. If you're not sure how you measure up, do a courtesy check for yourself and your staff — then start using polite, courteous service as a sales advantage to impress your customers. Soon you will notice that they are showing their appreciation by bringing new business through your doors and it's only a matter of time until you're head and shoulders above the competition. After all, who wouldn't want to do business with a company as nice as yours?

———•••———

I was in Hawaii speaking for the company H.Y. Louie at the Maui Prince Hotel and before turning in the night before, I asked for a 7 a.m. wake-up call to ensure that I would have time to prepare before my presentation. The next morning, I happened to awake at 5 a.m. and decided to go for a run. So, as it turned out, I wasn't in my room for the wake-up call.

Although I didn't know it at the time, when a guest doesn't answer their wake-up call, this hotel has a habit of continuing to phone back every five minutes for 15 minutes. Apparently, when I still didn't answer the subsequent calls, the staff member on duty became concerned. I returned to my room at 7:15 to find one of the staff knocking on the door to make sure that I was okay. Considering that the hotel had hundreds of other guests to attend to besides me, I thought that was pretty exceptional customer service.

———•••———

Using the phrase "thank you" is a powerful tool that we don't use often enough in business today. Late-night TV host Jay Leno once joked about this on a segment of his show when he relayed a story about a shopping experience he had had. After making a purchase, he told the clerk that she forgot to say thank you. To which she curtly responded, "It's printed on your receipt."

Talk about not making the customer feel appreciated.

Thankfully, there are many companies that genuinely care about their customers and want to help them . . . which reminds me of a story about a pharmacy that decided to turn an inconvenience into an advantage.

As it happened, this particular pharmacy's telephone number was very similar to the number of a nearby movie theatre. As you can expect, they got a lot of wrong numbers, mostly from people calling to ask what time the movie started.

For a long time, the pharmacy employees simply told callers they had the wrong number, until one day somebody came up with the idea to turn this minor but frequent annoyance into a win-win opportunity.

From then on, whenever someone called to ask about a movie, the pharmacy employee would say, "I'm sorry. This is the Walgreen's store just down the street from the movie theatre. But I have the schedule right here. What movie were you interested in?"

Once they had answered the caller's question, the pharmacy employee would then say, "When you finish the movie, you might consider coming over here. We have a great sale going on right now. I hope you enjoy the movie."

Instead of being irritated by 50 wrong calls each day, this store turned it into 50 promotions per day. They provided a small extra by giving out the movie schedule, but they got a fair amount of business in return.

A MASTER KNOWS: What we have done for ourselves alone dies with us; what we have done for others and the world remains and lives on.

In the following comments, a new member of our team, Accountant Joy Ginete, shares her perspective on what sets Canada Wide apart from other companies.

As a contract employee with Canada Wide Magazines for the last eight-and-a-half months, not only have I learned a great deal about their business and been able to enhance my skills professionally, I also have had the chance to meet and develop good relationships with people from many different backgrounds. People here love what they do and it is not just a matter of getting their paycheque every month. I can tell by the care that they take in performing their jobs that they think about the effect it will have on the company's bottom line and the future success of the business.

In my time here, I've been lucky to have the opportunity to work with the accounting dream team here at Canada Wide Magazines. Based on the experience I had with the past four companies I worked with, I always thought that the year-end financial process was a difficult, stressful time. However, despite the pressures the department is facing — with the implementation of a new global software system and new staff — the team here has never lost their enthusiasm or sense of humour in doing their jobs. I am so very impressed with how my colleagues Terri Mason, Jocelyn Snelling and Ruth Pisko deal with each of the accounts they are responsible for and how they always have the time to lend a hand or a brain, especially to a "newbie" like me.

Most companies expect their employees to go the extra mile in their performance and I think that's great, but what I notice here at Canada Wide is that the employees are willing not just to go one mile, they would go an extra hundred miles. This is especially evident after working closely with Assistant Controller Tammy Grinnell (no wonder she's the most recent recipient of the Bernie Legge employee-of-the-year award). Despite the short time that I have been here, it is very apparent to me that management appreciates their employees and never fails to encourage them. It is also no wonder that Canada Wide Magazines has been in business for the last 30 years, profitably and with a first-rate reputation.

Dealing with Personal Conflicts

In both your business and home life, nothing can destroy your sense of accomplishment and wellbeing faster than personal conflicts. Upsets between business partners or battles between bosses and staff ruin productivity, reduce income and build up the level of stress for everyone — especially those who get caught in the crossfire.

Conflicts at home, particularly those with a spouse, can spill over into your business life when you show up for work in a bad mood, overtired or distracted. Bad relationships at work are likewise damaging to your personal relationships when you come home feeling fed up and frustrated and take it out on your spouse, children, other family members or friends.

Most people have good intentions most of the time. They want to get along, do their best and succeed. Yet personal upsets can make otherwise good people difficult to be around. Office politics, backstabbing, rumours, jealousy and revenge are all the result of personal conflicts, and no matter which side of the argument you are on, it can be a major obstacle to your success.

Most relationship problems are the result of a breakdown in communication and the feeling of one or the other party that they are not being treated with respect.

Another story I've told before comes from the *New York Times* and it's about a fellow who had gone downtown to do a little shopping. Of course, New York, like many other big cities, is a very expensive place to park. So this guy stops in at his bank (where he thought that he was a valued customer) to have them validate his parking ticket. When he gets up to the teller with his request, the teller tells him in a snarky tone of voice that they only validate parking tickets for customers who are conducting a business transaction. The fellow thinks about this for a moment and then he says to the teller, "Very well, please close my account . . . and then you can validate my parking ticket."

As a result, the customer moved his million-dollar account to the bank across the street — where I'm pretty sure that they didn't have any problem validating his parking tickets.

It's not easy facing up to conflict; for many of us, it feels like failure when our interactions with others aren't pleasant or productive. Generally, conflict arises when at least one party feels that they aren't getting what they want or need out of the interaction. The longer this goes on, the more the relationship deteriorates until the person in question is either too angry to make an effort, or worse still, completely indifferent.

Here are four steps that can be useful in resolving any personal conflict, whether at home or in the workplace:

1. *Open up a line of communication.* Often when conflict arises, it is either because one party feels that they are not being heard or they feel that the other party is unapproachable. You can open up a line of communication by telling the other party in a direct way that you would like to work on improving your relationship with them.

2. *Establish some common ground.* With busy schedules and multiple responsibilities, it is easy for miscommunication to happen. Clarifying both parties' assumptions/understanding of the situation is an important step towards resolution.

3. *Discover what is wanted and/or needed from both parties* and agree on what changes can be made to fulfill those

wants/needs. Sometimes we let others down for the simple reason that we don't know what they want or need from us. Likewise, they may not be living up to our expectations because we have not communicated them clearly.

It is not always easy to express what we want and need from others, especially in situations where others may have authority over us. However, it is essential if we want to have productive relationships. The best way to approach this is to ask the other party to tell you their wants and needs first and then you can reciprocate with your own.

4. *Act on fulfilling the agreement.* While the three previous steps have been focused on clearing the air and establishing expectations, this step is the first one towards rebuilding the relationship. That's why it is so important to follow through on your commitment, making the changes you agreed to and maintaining open communication with the other party.

The above steps can also be used as a proactive approach for establishing rapport with new employees, customers, co-workers, bosses and associates. If you're skeptical about how effective it would be, just imagine how you would feel if the new CEO of the company you work for invited you into his or her office and said, "Thank you for taking the time to speak with me. I'd really like us to have a good working relationship right from the start, so why don't you tell me what you want and need from the company and from me as CEO."

CHAPTER 12

*"You are not here merely to make a living.
You are here to enable the world to live more
amply, with greater vision and a finer
spirit of hope and achievement. You are here
to enrich the world. You impoverish yourself
if you forget this errand."*

— Woodrow Wilson

Masterpiece Tool:
Serve the Community

While there may be nearly as many reasons to serve the community
as there are ways to serve it, by far the strongest and most enduring
among these is love of the place you call home . . . whether it be a
particular street, neighbourhood, city, or as was the case with
James F. MacDonald, inlet.

James MacDonald, or "Mac" to everyone he met, first set eyes
on the inlet in question in 1919. He was a young man at the time
and from the first moment he saw it, he fell in love with Princess
Louisa Inlet. Needing to earn a living, Mac spent the next six or
seven years prospecting in the Southern U.S. After striking it rich
in Nevada in 1927, Mac immediately returned to buy 45 acres of
land surrounding Chatterbox Falls at the head of the inlet. There he
built himself a log cabin and made it his home.

For years, Mac acted as host to visiting yachtsmen and sailors, telling everyone who visited that "this beautiful, peaceful haven should never belong to one individual." Mac never wanted to see the inlet used for commercial purposes. In his opinion, he was simply a custodian for Nature and it was his duty to extend every courtesy to those who visited.

In 1953, Mac turned the title to Princess Louisa Inlet over to the boating public in trust and the Princess Louisa International Society was formed to preserve this beautiful treasure in its pristine state for future generations. In the trust, it was stipulated that Mac would always have a place near Chatterbox Falls to moor his houseboat and he continued to spend much time there until 1972 (when he spent his last summer at the inlet). For the last five or six years of his life, Mac was unable to return to Princess Louisa Inlet. He died in 1978, having lived to be almost 90 years old.

Ten years after the Princess Louisa International Society was formed, a decision was made with Mac's blessing, to give the property over to the care of the Government of British Columbia. In accordance with all of the provisions that were already in place, the property became the Princess Louisa Provincial Marine Park in 1965.

To this day, the inlet remains as beautiful as it ever was, thanks to Mac and his generous spirit. You see, Mac could have sold his property in 1953 (he was offered $400,000, which was a fortune at that time) and retired a very wealthy man. Instead, he chose to ensure that this masterpiece of nature would always remain untouched and pristine for everyone to enjoy.

For those who have never visited the area, the famous writer Erle Stanley Gardner describes Princess Louisa Inlet perfectly in his book, *Log of a Landlubber*. He writes:

There is no use describing that inlet. Perhaps an atheist

could view it and remain an atheist, but I doubt it. There is a calm tranquility which stretches from the smooth surface of the reflecting water straight up into infinity. The deep calm of eternal silence is disturbed only by the muffled roar of throbbing waterfalls as they plunge down from sheer cliffs.

There is no scenery in the world that can beat it. Not that I've seen the rest of the world. I don't need to, I've seen Princess Louisa Inlet.

Every day showed some new glimpse of nature. Constantly changing clouds clung to the sheer cliffs for companionship, drifting lightly from crag to crag, lazily floating along above their swimming reflections giving ever new light combinations, ever new contours. Clouds, water, trees, mountains, snow and sky all seem to be perpetually the same through the countless ages of eternal time, and yet to be changing hourly. One views the scenery with bared head and choking feeling of the throat. It is more than beautiful. It is sacred.

Having spent some summers in Princess Louisa Inlet myself, I had the opportunity to meet Mac on a number of occasions, although I never imagined that I would one day be asked to conduct his memorial service, but that is exactly what happened.

The first few times our paths crossed, I was a teenager attending a Young Life Christian summer camp called Malibu (it was originally built in the late 1930s by aviation tycoon Tom Hamilton, who invented the variable pitch propeller, as a wilderness playground for Hollywood starlets and millionaires) that has been operating at the mouth of Princess Louisa Inlet since the early 1950s.

In those summers of my youth, we kids knew him as Mac of the Princess, and once a week he would come over from his place at Chatterbox Falls to talk to us and tell stories about his life in the wilderness and the area's First Nations history. You could tell by his enthusiasm that nobody loved the inlet more than Mac, and to us he was as much a part of the Princess as the trees and the water.

As a funny turn of fate, I ended up returning to Malibu in the late '70s to work as the camp manager. With 300 people in the camp, I was in charge of making sure everything was running smoothly. It was on one particular Saturday when I began to notice all kinds of boats coming into the inlet and passing by the camp on their way to Chatterbox Falls.

Just as the property manager, Don Prettie, and I were walking out onto the dock to check it out, a gentleman stepped off his boat and to our utter surprise, declared loudly, "I'm looking for a preacher."

"What on earth do you need a preacher for?" asked Don, who was just as curious as I.

"We're planning to bury Mac's ashes up at Chatterbox Falls and tomorrow we'll have a service for all of his friends, admirers and members of the Princess Louisa Society," he explained.

"Well, we don't have a preacher," offered Don, "but Peter here is a Christian speaker and he could perform the service for you."

Not knowing exactly what I was getting into (or why Don had so readily volunteered my services), I agreed to do it and that night I sat up late, preparing my comments for the following day.

Sunday was a cool, rainy day and when it was time for me to leave for the memorial, Don took me up to Chatterbox Falls in the camp's speedboat. We disembarked on the shore to a waiting crowd of about 300 people standing in the pouring rain.

I performed my duties to the best of my ability that day,

speaking of Mac's love of the inlet and his dedication to preserving it. When the service was over, we said our goodbyes and headed back to the camp. On the way back in the boat, Don turned to me and said, "You know, Peter, you need to stop speaking just to kids. After hearing your words today, I think you need to start doing talks for adults because you had those 300 people riveted with your message."

In some way, I owe the discovery of my talent as a motivational speaker to Mac of the Princess and the best way I know to honour the memory of Mac is to continue to give to the community just as he did. In fact, this June I will be returning to Princess Louisa Inlet to speak at a celebration weekend at Malibu.

Speaking on that same weekend will be Bob Mitchell, a man for whom I have great admiration. Bob was a speaker at the camp when I was in high school. I never would have dreamed as a kid sitting on the floor listening to Bob, that one day some 45 years later I would be up there sharing the stage with him.

You never know how an event will cause your life to change . . . or what new insight it may offer into the masterpiece you were meant to create.

———•••———

I am happy to devote a good portion of my time and talent every year to some very important causes that I believe in. Among them are Variety — The Children's Charity, the Heart and Stroke Foundation, Young Life and the Salvation Army. As much as I give to them, however, I feel that I get even more in return in terms of the smiling faces and countless displays of appreciation that I receive. I have also been very fortunate in my life to have strong role models (like my father) and great mentors like Ray Addington, Mel Cooper and Joe Segal, who showed me by example the importance of community service. So I was surprised one day at lunch when Joe turned to me and said, "You know, Peter, you could be 10 times more successful than you are in business, but you apply much of your time and energy to serving the community."

I simply looked right back at him and said, "I wonder where I learned that from!"

I've never met anyone who gives more than Joe, and that giving has, in turn, encouraged many others to give of themselves. Joe told me a story recently about a young man who once sent him a letter with a $50 bill in it. In the letter, the fellow asked Joe if he would have lunch with him and give him some advice. Joe agreed to the request and they set a day and time for the meeting.

At the lunch, Joe shook the young man's hand and returned his $50. When they sat down to eat, the young man explained his predicament. "Joe," he said. "I want to be successful like you, I want to make a lot of money, but I don't have a lot of money right now to invest. What should I do?"

Joe could see that the young man was both serious and ambitious, so he gave him the following advice, "If you want to make a lot of money, I would suggest that you either get into working in the stock market or go into real estate. You don't need capital for either of these careers, you just need the willingness for hard work, long hours and the discipline to learn the business. "

The lunch ended and each man went his separate way.

Some years later, the young man showed up at the new Segal School of Business at Simon Fraser University (Joe, his wife Rosalie and their family bought the old Bank of Montreal building in downtown Vancouver and donated it to the university) just before it was set to open its doors for the first time. Joe heard about the young man's visit and wanted to give him a personal tour of the school from top to bottom.

As they walked from floor to floor and room to room, the young man revealed to Joe just how well the advice that he had given him had paid off. The young man was indeed a success and had heard that a couple of the lecture rooms still needed sponsoring in time for the grand opening.

The young man settled on a $200,000 sponsorship of one of the rooms on the second floor. It was his way of saying thank you to Joe for taking the time to meet, listen and offer some thoughtful advice.

Such is the life and generosity of Joe Segal.

A MASTER KNOWS: At the end of the day, our legacy will be how many people we've helped and how well we've left this world after we've gone from it.

There are so many ways in which service to the community pays dividends, not least of which is the feeling you get when you are able to bring happiness to someone. That was certainly the case a few years ago when Air Canada and Variety — The Children's Charity took a couple of children with chronic health problems on a trip to Disneyland for a special treat.

To capture the occasion to share with sponsors and donors, Variety had taken along a video camera. Throughout the day, the two children and their families visited almost every attraction in the park without one smile or sign of enjoyment from the children. It was nearly time for them to leave to catch their flight home and everyone was feeling a little disappointed when suddenly Mickey Mouse came around the corner and stopped right in front of the children to greet them.

I can tell you it was as if someone had flipped a switch to

watch how those two little faces lit up with happiness and joy.

———•·•———

When you find a cause that you believe in, support it in every way that you can: your time, your talent, your energy and even money.

CHAPTER 13

*"The man who does things makes many
mistakes, but he never makes the biggest mistake
of all — doing nothing."*
— Benjamin Franklin

Masterpiece Tool:
Turn Your Errors into Advantages

Back in 1985, Ray Addington, who is one of my mentors, asked
me to be involved with him in the promotion of the British Pavilion
at Expo 86 in Vancouver. I jumped at the opportunity. The biggest
part of the job at hand was to find corporate sponsors who were
willing to help fund the pavilion in return for promotional exposure
at the exposition.

To find sponsors, we put together a promotional package and a
group of us went over to London, England, to sell these packages
bringing along an Expo 86 audiovisual presentation to show to all
the British companies that might be persuaded to participate in
encouraging people to visit the British Pavilion.

We had a variety of sponsorship packages for sale, each one
named after a district of London. As I recall, there was a Mayfair
package (this one was the most expensive), a Piccadilly package, a
Leicester Square package and a few others. Each package was
priced based on the district for which it was named and featured a
list of benefits that the sponsoring company would receive in return

for their investment. These included media time, magazine space, logos and the like.

When we were on the plane and in the air — we flew on British Airways, I might add — the group had a meeting to review the package offerings and our sales pitch. In reviewing the brochures that had been custom printed for the occasion, we discovered — to our great and collective horror — that the word Piccadilly had been misspelled. By this point in time, there was absolutely no way we could have the brochures reprinted in time for the presentation and we could hardly reschedule the presentation to a later date. Therefore, we did the only thing we could do; we came up with a scheme to turn our error into an advantage.

Here's how it worked out.

Through the British trade association, we had invited all of these big companies to come to a presentation where I was to be the master of ceremonies. We started off the program by playing an audiovisual presentation about Expo 86 in order to familiarize everyone with the transportation theme of the fair. Following that, we prepared to hand out the brochures that explained the sponsorship packages available. At this point, rather than try to cover up our spelling mistake or apologize for it, we announced that we had purposely misspelled one of the place names within the brochure and the first person to find it would win a prize.

To be sure, every single representative in the audience that day began scouring the material thoroughly to spot the deliberate error and it wasn't long before we had a winner.

I'm happy to say that as a result of our creative approach to problem-solving, we turned what could have been an embarrassing disaster into a great opportunity. And to top it off, we sold every one of those sponsorship packages. I think that's what makes the real difference between people who are successful and those who aren't —

the willingness to look at a problem and see the opportunity within it.

———•—•———

The Royal Palace of Tehran in Iran contains what is undoubtedly one of the most beautiful mosaic masterpieces in the world. The interior walls and ceiling sparkle with multifaceted reflections as if encrusted with thousands upon thousands of diamonds. However, this vision of beauty is not quite as it was intended to be.

When the palace was first designed, the architect in charge specified that huge sheets of mirrors should hang on the walls. Unfortunately, when the first shipment of mirrors arrived from Paris, the builders found that the glass had been shattered in transit. The contractor in charge promptly threw the mirrors into the trash and sadly informed the architect of the problem.

To the surprise of the builders, the architect did not despair at this news. Instead, he ordered that all of the broken pieces be collected together and brought to him. The architect then proceeded to smash the glass into even smaller pieces before ordering that the pieces be glued onto the walls, creating a mosaic of shimmering bits of glass.

Obviously, the architect had the eye of an artist to be able to take something broken and turn it into a beautiful masterpiece. However, there is another lesson to be gleaned from the story, and it is this: If we simply choose to see it from a different angle, what looks like an obstacle can in fact become a glorious opportunity.

———•—•———

A MASTER KNOWS: There are only two real mistakes a person can make along the road to success: not going all the way and not starting.

———··——

Here are some tips on how you can turn obstacles into opportunity:

- **Accept responsibility**. You don't have to admit to the whole world that you made a mistake, but you do have to admit it to yourself and anyone else that will be affected by it — and the sooner the better. Also, never use your authority to mask a mistake. If you make one, admit it, explain it, apologize for it and above all else, learn from it. Allowing others to see how you accept responsibility and learn from your errors can go a long way towards healing any loss of faith.
- **Ask for help**. If you're determined to fly solo through every storm, eventually you're going to crash and burn. But it doesn't have to be that way; it's all up to you. Sometimes, a fresh perspective — especially from someone who doesn't have an emotional attachment to the problem — is just what you need to get things moving forward again. So don't be afraid to ask for input and use it to your advantage.
- **Don't overanalyze your errors**. Despite the fact that you made a mistake, there is no need to wallow in endless rounds of coulda, shoulda, woulda. Once you admit that you've made an error, look to the future. What have you learned? How will you keep from making the same mistake again? Where do you go from here?
- **Don't be afraid to laugh at your mistakes**. The ability to see humour in a problem can make the lesson it has to teach us much more palatable. Former NBA centre and coach Johnny Kerr tells a story about the time when he was

coaching the Chicago Bulls. At the time, Kerr was struggling with the challenges of coaching an expansion team and in the midst of a major losing streak, he tried to pump up the team by giving them a pre-game pep talk before they headed out onto the floor in Boston.

"We had lost seven in a row and I decided to give a psychological pep talk before a game with the Celtics," Kerr explains.

During the talk, Kerr told Bob Boozer to pretend he was the best scorer in basketball, he told Jerry Sloan to pretend he could stop anyone in the game, then he told Guy Rodgers to pretend he was the top point guard in the league, and finally, he told six-foot-eight Erwin Mueller to pretend he was a shot-blocking, rebounding machine.

"We played the Celtics at the Garden and lost by 17 points," Kerr recalls. "So I was pacing around the locker room afterward, trying to figure out what to say to the team when Mueller walked up, put his arm around me and said, 'Don't worry about it, coach. Just pretend we won.' "

- **Use the difficulty**. When legendary actor Michael Caine was asked what fatherly advice he had for his children, he relayed the story of a direction he had been given by a theatre producer early in his career. The situation in question took place when Caine was rehearsing with other actors and found himself waiting behind a door for his cue to come onstage during a scene in which a couple were having an argument.

As the scene progressed, the actors started throwing furniture around and a chair became lodged in front of the door. When Caine was cued, he found that he couldn't open the door to make his entrance.

"I can't get in!" he shouted, breaking character. "The chair's in the way."

Without hesitation, the producer turned to Caine and told him, "Use the difficulty."

Confused, Caine asked the director just what he meant.

"Well," the producer explained, "If it's a drama, pick the chair up and smash it. If it's a comedy, fall over it."

Caine said the point was not lost on him and the idea stuck in his mind.

"I taught it to my children," he revealed. "That with any situation in life that's negative, there is something positive you can do with it."

———•◦•———

"To err is human, but when the eraser wears out ahead of the pencil, you're overdoing it."

— Josh Jenkins

CHAPTER 14

*"Everyone thinks of changing the world, but
no one thinks of changing himself."*
— Leo Tolstoy

Masterpiece Tool:
Staying Fit

As my friend Dr. Art Hister, who has a program on CKNW radio in Vancouver, is fond of saying, "If you don't make the time for exercise now, you'd better leave time for illness later."

These days, I'm very proactive in my health regimen and I attribute it to two things. The first is the stroke I had a few years ago, which was really a wake-up call about how I was treating my body, including my habits around eating, sleeping, working and most of all, exercise. The rest of the credit goes to my last book, *The Runway of Life*. As I was writing that book, I started thinking about how my own runway would someday end and of all the things that I still want to accomplish in my life.

I realized that I can't wait until I'm 80 to start taking care of myself. I need to ensure that my body is as healthy as it can be so that I can make it to 80 in the first place. If I want to have any hope of being able to do all of the things that I want to do and have the energy that I'll need to do them, I have to look after myself as best I can starting right now.

Although it is not always easy to fit a healthy lifestyle into running a business, there are some basic habits to which I always try to adhere.

First of all, no matter if I am at home or away, I usually get to bed by nine or ten o'clock every evening. Sometimes this can be a challenge when I have evening engagements to attend, but whoever said that you have to stay until the end of every party? Not me. When I go to a cocktail party or reception, I focus on three important tasks: first, I show up (in a timely fashion); secondly, I seek out the person who invited me and thank them for their hospitality; thirdly, I mingle and meet a few people (exchanging business cards), and then I'm done.

My early-to-bed policy also accounts for the success of my annual charity golf tournament, which always ends by 7 p.m. Even if it is for a good cause, in my experience very few people want to spend all day on the golf course and then have to sit through an awards dinner that cuts into their family time.

My second habit involves exercise. While maintaining a regular exercise regimen has always been one of my biggest challenges, I've been much more successful since I dedicated a room in my home as a gym. In my gym I have a variety of equipment including a treadmill, stationary bicycle and rowing machine. I've been able to discipline myself so that on at least four out of seven days I exercise for 30 to 45 minutes before leaving for work. I like to keep track of how many miles I do every day and I mix up my routine from day to day with a total of 15 different kinds of exercises.

My last habit focuses on eating a more sensible diet (i.e., cutting out the crap!). What I've noticed in regards to my diet is that in many cases, it is the little changes that make the most difference (because they are the ones that I can actually stick with) over the long term. One such change that I have made is to eat oatmeal for breakfast six days each week. This has had a very positive effect on my cholesterol level and by allowing myself one day per week to still have more indulgent foods such as bacon or eggs benedict, I don't feel as though I am being deprived.

I'm also changing the way that I eat at business functions. Some people see a meal out as an excuse to break their diet, but you can choose not to fall into that trap. When you go to a banquet, you can generally have a good meal, but that doesn't mean you always have to give in to the most indulgent foods on offer. If decadent sweets happen to be your downfall, before the main course is over, ask the server to bring you a fruit plate. That way it will be in front of you when it is time for dessert as a gentle reminder of your healthy eating strategy.

Something else that is important for everyone (especially when you reach a certain age) is to make time for an annual medical examination and regular dental appointments. Although it's easy to let these slip (after all, who likes being poked and prodded?), remember that the majority of serious medical conditions can be successfully treated if the early warning signs are detected and acted upon.

A MASTER KNOWS: It's not easy to start living healthier, but it is important if you want to be around to finish the masterpiece you've started.

Here are some healthy living tips that may come in handy:

1. Many busy people find that a personal trainer is a good investment in their health (especially when they are just

starting out on an exercise program), since they tend to know the latest trends and can teach you how to exercise safely. If you choose to go this route, make sure you choose a certified professional.

2. The real secret to success is not to set yourself up for failure. Deciding that you're going to get in shape as of January 1 doesn't work. You've got to make a mental decision that you want to be healthier and then you have to make a commitment to yourself that over the next two, three or four years, you're going to take a more healthy approach to all aspects of your life.

3. Statistically speaking, if you smoke, you're going to die early. So if you smoke, do everything you can to help yourself quit.

4. No drugs of any kind unless they have been prescribed for a specific purpose (for obvious reasons).

5. Eat protein at every meal. Unlike high-carbohydrate foods that provide quick energy but leave you feeling hungry soon after, high-protein foods help ward off hunger between meals — which can keep you from snacking. Lean protein sources include meat, fish, turkey, chicken, string cheese, non-fat yogurt, cottage cheese and natural peanut butter.

6. Don't eat "white" at night. The white in question refers to potatoes, rice, bread and other processed starches (including most desserts). These are all high-carb foods that are basically converted to sugar and have no real nutritional value. White foods are better eaten early in the day while your body is active and more able to burn off the extra energy.

7. Simply choose to eat less. One of the simplest and most effective changes we can make to improve our diet is to eat less. However, exercising portion control is a challenge for

most of us because we take an all-or-nothing approach when it comes to putting food on our plate — we either indulge to excess or starve ourselves of all the foods we like to indulge in until our cravings get the better of us. Wouldn't it be far more practical to have a little bit of the foods we like, along with the healthier foods we know our bodies need?

And a few more tips:

1. If you love chocolate, choose to eat dark chocolate (the less processed, the better), which is full of heart-healthy flavonoids that act as anti-oxidants. Just make sure that you limit yourself to one or two squares rather than eating the whole bar.

2. Beware of fancy coffee drinks (such as mocha frappuccinos) and gourmet ice cream if you are trying to cut down on calories. Both are full of sugar and fat. Instead of ice cream, try eating sorbet, which has virtually no fat and comes in a variety of fruit flavours, both mild and wild.

3. Rather than cutting foods like cheese (which is very high in fat) out of your diet, try changing the types you are using and the way you serve them. Rather than eating cheese in slices, try grating a small amount over whatever you would normally eat it with.

4. Eat more often. It may sound crazy to anyone who is cutting back on their calorie intake in order to lose weight, but when we don't eat, our bodies go into starvation mode and our metabolism slows down to conserve energy. Recent studies confirm that eating smaller meals every three to four hours is more effective at sustaining metabolism and aiding long-term weight loss than skipping meals or restricting ourselves to a strict low-calorie diet.

5. Get enough sleep. Research shows that people who don't get enough sleep (seven to eight hours a night) are more prone to weight gain. This is because sleep deprivation puts more stress on our nervous system. Additionally, we now know that lean muscle is regenerated in the final couple of hours of sleep each night, so if you don't get the zzz's you need, you're actually weakening your body.

6. Walk the dog. Here's a helpful idea for people who have difficulty sticking to an exercise program or keeping their weight at a healthy level. A study at the University of Missouri-Columbia showed that simply taking a dog for a walk on a regular basis was more effective over a one-year period than other major weight-loss programs. In the study, researchers had participants begin by walking a dog for 10 minutes a day three days a week, building up to 20 minutes a day five days a week. By the end of a year, they found that the dog walkers lost an average of 14 pounds and because they were actually interacting with the dog (as opposed to running on a treadmill or walking alone), they were more motivated to stick with the exercise program for the long term. So even if you don't have a dog of your own, borrow a neighbour's dog and get walking.

7. Avoid stress. Lastly, and most important of all, get your stress under control. Both physical and emotional stress can cause our bodies to release cortisol, a steroid that slows down the metabolism. When your metabolism slows, your body automatically begins to store more fat, causing you to gain weight, particularly around the tummy.

CHAPTER 15

"People who are funny and smart and return phone calls get much better press than people who are just funny and smart."

— Howard Simons

Masterpiece Tool:
Return Phone Calls

Some tools of success are simpler than others. Although the tool that I am going to focus on in this chapter is one of the simplest, it is also one of the most effective in building your credibility with others. It is the art of returning telephone calls (and emails, letters and replies to invitations or proposals) in a timely manner.

"What is a reasonable amount of time?" you ask. I would suggest 24 hours.

Steve Halliday, General Manager and Vice President of the Pan Pacific Hotel Vancouver, has a couple of similar habits that he shared with me recently:

1. The 10-Foot Rule. Whenever Steve is in the hotel and around guests, he makes a habit of making eye contact with and acknowledging every customer within a 10-foot radius of himself. This simple technique has a powerful impact on customers, as it demonstrates in a very active way that they are more than just a room number to the management and staff of the hotel.

2. First-Ring Rule. Another habit that sets Steve apart from so many other top-level executives is his practice of picking up and answering the telephone on the first ring whenever possible. It's not rocket science, but it is very, very effective. "Anyone who wants to make customers feel more valued should try practising this rule," advises Steve.

———•—•———

A MASTER KNOWS: To always return calls from the media, even if it is to say that you are unable to answer their questions at the present moment. Otherwise they may publish or broadcast a message that says: "So-and-so did not return our calls."

———•—•———

Because we spend so much of our time communicating over the telephone, here are eight more strategies for making the most of your communications:

1. When you answer the phone, greet callers with energy and enthusiasm. Given that the first few words out of your mouth will set the tone for the conversation, make sure that the image you are projecting is positive and professional.

2. Ask for the caller's name if he or she doesn't offer it. Use their name during the first few moments of your conversation, then one or two more times during the call (just don't overdo it or you'll risk sounding phony) and end by thanking the caller by name.

3. Take brief notes during your telephone conversation if you will need the information for future reference. People are impressed when you can recall important details later on; likewise, they can feel harassed if they need to recall the same details time after time.

4. Sit up tall, smile and use gestures when you are speaking. Callers can hear your smile and they can also hear your slouch. Practising good posture helps you breathe better and stay alert during the conversation.

5. To build rapport with a caller, match the pace of your speech with theirs. If you are hearing long silences, it probably means you are speaking too quickly. Use pauses effectively to slow down so the caller can follow what you're saying.

6. Use professional but conversational vocabulary and grammar. Avoid using industry jargon unless you are sure the caller shares your knowledge of it, and definitely stay away from swearing or slang.

7. Before you put someone on hold or transfer their call, ask permission from the caller. Small courtesies like these help to build rapport and enhance your image.

8. End the call with sincere thanks and appreciation for the caller's time. Be positive and courteous, especially if the caller discussed a problem or complaint. Focus on positive results.

Not being afraid to make a call to go after what you want is also important to your success in life. Here is a story from Laurel MacLean, one of Canada Wide's art directors, on how she did just that.

My story isn't as desperate as the one Anya Lewis tells in Chapter 7. I didn't have to go chasing VP of Production Corinne Smith into a public bathroom to give her my résumé! I simply called and asked to make an appointment with her, to show her a fantastic portfolio with overseas work. I decided to skip the part that I was five months pregnant — and just take my chances.

The interview went well, so I then mentioned I was pregnant, but interested in freelancing until my baby was due and would like to return to work as soon as possible after the baby was born, if we were both happy with things.

Corinne called a couple of days later to have me start designing advertising with Advertising Art Director Marianne Carr, who immediately took me under her wing. Afterwards, when my daughter was only six weeks old and I'd become a very sleep-deprived young mom, I received a call from Corinne wondering when I could return to work!

CHAPTER 16

*"She wants me to dress smart-casual.
What is that?"*

"I don't know, but you don't have it."

— Characters George and Jerry in a scene
from the TV show *Seinfeld*

Masterpiece Tool:
Dress Smartly

A number of years ago, a teenager by the name of Jacqueline
Rogers took a job at Canada Wide working with our former editor
Bonnie Irving doing filing, research and circulation work for
BCBusiness magazine. During her days here, she always wore jeans
and a T-shirt, but from the outset, I was impressed with her positive
attitude, her boundless energy and her enthusiasm, and often
wondered how she would fare in sales. One day I decided to find out
so I asked Jacquie if she would make a couple of sales calls.

Her answer was a very firm no, and at the time I didn't
understand her reluctance.

It wasn't until a few weeks later that I discovered the real
reason for her answer. The only clothes that Jacquie owned were
jeans and T-shirts and she didn't feel that this was a suitable
wardrobe for someone who was making sales calls. I also

discovered that she had absolutely no money to buy new clothes, so I handed her a cheque for $1,000 and asked her to go to the mall and buy three or four inexpensive but smart outfits.

Jacquie bought the clothes that she needed and went on the sales calls. Just as I suspected, she was a natural and it was the beginning of a whole new career for her here at Canada Wide Magazines. Today, Jacquie Rogers is Retail Sales Manager of *TV Week*, bringing that same energy, passion and excitement that I first recognized to all that she does.

———

How you dress defines your business presence and to those who don't know you, you are how you dress. As a general rule of thumb, in new situations you have just four seconds to make a first impression.

According to Michelle Sterling, an image consultant and founder of Global Image Group, the process works like this:

- If you appear to be on a comparable business or social level, you are considered suitable for further interaction.
- If you appear to be of higher business or social status, you are admired and cultivated as a valuable contact.
- If you appear to be of lower business or social standing, you are tolerated but kept at arm's length.
- If you are in an interview situation, you can either appear to match the corporate culture or not, something that will ultimately affect the outcome of your career path.

Which of these categories do you want to be in?

———

A MASTER KNOWS: You don't dress for the job you have now. You dress for the job you want to have.

———•—•———

Knowing how to dress in an ever-changing business world can be a challenge. Searching on the Internet for clarification on how to dress for business occasions can be a lot like trying to file your own income taxes. One site I visited that claimed to demystify the term "business casual" offered no fewer than six different categories of dress, among them: active casual, smart casual, dressy casual and my favourite, power casual. However, in reading the clothing descriptions given for each category, the distinction between one type of casual and another was lost on me.

That's why, when it comes to deciding how to dress for any business occasion, I like to keep it simple. My rule of thumb is always to dress just a little bit better than the person you are going to meet, particularly if they are a client and you are making a sales call. That is, if you know that your client prefers to wear dress pants and a shirt with the top button undone, you should choose either a suit or coordinated slacks (or skirt for women) and jacket (men should have a tie) to give yourself a more professional look.

———•—•———

A MASTER KNOWS: No one ever lost a sale for looking too professional.

———•—•———

Here are five tips to help you dress smartly:
1. Too many patterns or textures can mess up your look, so don't wear stripes or checks on both your shirt and pants. Reserve a texture or pattern either for your top or bottom, and keep the other plain. Team a patterned tie with a plain shirt.

2. No matter what you wear, your clothes should always be neat, clean and in good condition. Remember, even casual attire should never look sloppy or worn out.

3. Don't forget to look down. Your shoes should be in good condition and of a type that is appropriate to the situation. Also, check that your heels are cleaned and in good condition. After you say goodbye, people will look at them as you walk away.

4. Invest in a good-quality wardrobe. If you don't have a lot of money to spend, focus on the basics first — slacks (skirts), dress shirts (blouses) and shoes — and remember that you can never go wrong with black. It's always appropriate, versatile for all seasons and it works with all other colours.

5. You're not dressed for business unless you have your business cards on you. Always try to have a small pocket somewhere on your person to carry a few business cards that are easily accessible — because you never know who you're going to meet.

CHAPTER 17

"The meaning of life is to find your gift, the purpose of life is to give it away."

— Joy J. Golliver

Masterpiece Tool:
Focus on Your Own Unique Talent

In my early days as a beginner on the public speaking circuit, Earl Nightingale once told me, "If you are able to master the art of platform speaking, the doors of opportunity that open for you will dwarf your imagination."

I thought at the time, "Yeah sure, that's okay for you, Earl, but it would never happen to me." Looking back now some 25 years later, I had no idea how right Earl would be.

Over the years, I have invested an enormous amount of time to study other speakers and hone my own skills as a speaker. As I have mentioned in earlier books, the way that I established myself was by being willing to speak the first 500 times for free. As each year goes by, that investment continues to pay off in ways that I never imagined it would. Recently, John Furlong asked me to be one of 18 ambassadors for Vancouver's 2010 Olympic Games. I can't tell you how honoured I am to be asked, and I couldn't be more proud to represent this region of our country to the world.

A MASTER KNOWS: When your passion and your talent intersect, you are unstoppable.

———•◦•———

When I was young, a speaking coach watched my presentation and later approached me to say, "You may not know it, but I think you could be the Elvis Presley of speaking. When he was starting out in his career, he didn't know what he had . . . and neither do you."

Despite the fact that they sounded a bit trite, I have to say that his words stuck with me and gave me encouragement to keep developing my own unique style on the podium. Although I don't seem to make the women in the audience swoon, I do have a talent for motivating people, something that — ego aside — is infinitely more satisfying.

———•◦•———

"You become what you think about most of the time."
— Earl Nightingale

———•◦•———

Throughout my younger life, and especially when I first started in business, my dad often said to me, "Don't accept either success or failure because neither need be permanent." I never dreamed that I would end up being the No. 1 awarded speaker in Canada or a member of the Speaker's Roundtable (a select networking group of 20 of the very best speakers in the world). I remember times over the years, when, in the course of developing my skill and making presentations in one small town after another across the country, I would wonder to myself, "When is this really going to pay off, when will I know that I have achieved success?"

What I didn't grasp during those years was that all of this

experience was adding up and I was building a strong foundation that would allow me to move to the next level in my career. On the other hand, what was beginning to dawn on me was that even with a jam-packed speaking schedule, I couldn't get in front of everyone in person. It was at this point that I decided to write a book and share my message with even more people.

My first book, *How to Soar with the Eagles*, was well received and this encouraged me to continue to write others, including my most recent book, *The Runway of Life* and three volumes of collected inspirational quotes titled *If Only I'd Said That*.

I have also been fortunate in the opportunities and recognition that my career as a speaker has brought. I am thankful for the experience of speaking:

- on five different continents;
- at a Prayer Breakfast in the House of Commons;
- before the U.S. Ambassador, Paul Cellucci;
- at Government House in Victoria.

I am grateful to the professional speaking community for conferring upon me the Certified Speaking Professional (CSP) designation, honouring me with the coveted Council of Peers Award of Excellence (CPAE) and inducting me into the Speakers Hall of Fame. I am indebted to Toastmasters International for presenting me with its highest honour, the Golden Gavel Award, and naming me one of the top five speakers in North America.

Frank Palmer, who is the head of DDB Advertising, said to me not so long ago, "If you start getting awards, look out, it means you must be nearing the end of your career." I don't see it that way. I plan on continuing to do what I do as long as I can. In fact, I'm working harder today than I did at any other time in my life. Two years ago I didn't have a marketing manager to promote my speaking engagements and a year ago I didn't even have a web site to highlight my services.

I know by what I do — having essentially two different careers — that I am infinitely more successful than the average business person. Although, neither the magazine business nor the speaking business will make you rich overnight — they are both very profitable in the long term and they have provided well for my family. However, what is in many ways even more satisfying than the money is knowing that my work has made a difference to others. It is very touching to know that I have had an impact on so many lives. This past year at Christmas, I was surprised at the number of cards I received with a similar message telling me that I had inspired or motivated someone to change their life in a way that had really made a difference to their success and well-being.

Sometimes I wonder about what people will remember about me when I'm gone. Here's what I hope they would say:

- He stayed married to the same lady all of his life.
- He had a tremendous relationship with his three daughters.
- He spent an extraordinary amount of time, effort and money supporting a variety of community-oriented organizations and programs.
- He was a person of honour and he did what he said he was going to do to the very best of his ability . . . he followed through.
- He ran a pretty damn fine company and built it from nothing almost overnight. Okay, well, maybe it took 30 years, but it seemed like it was overnight.
- He believed in tithing.
- He always had a positive attitude.
- He was an encourager of people.

*"Keep away from people who try to belittle your ambitions.
Small people always do that, but the really great make you feel
that you, too, can become great."*

— Mark Twain

———

Bee Fioraso, who is the Systems Administrator with Canada Wide, has her own story about choosing the career path that was right for her.

Have you ever wondered if the paths you take in life will finally take you somewhere? All my life I heard that everything happens for a reason. In my case, it did in the year 2001. At the time, I had come to a fork in the road, torn between whether I should pursue my current studies in criminology and a career in policing or try to get into what I seemed to have a natural passion for, computers.

Mostly, the thing that was holding me back was fear of the unknown, so I finally bit the bullet and quit the two jobs that had been providing me with a stable income and took out student loans to get myself into a full-time, 12-month course in Information Technology at the British Columbia Institute of Technology. I had absolutely no idea where this path would take me (with the recent dot-com bust, it was anyone's guess where the market was headed); all I knew was that I finally truly enjoyed what I was doing with my life.

That was more than four years ago now. Through my BCIT program, I accepted a work-term position at Canada Wide Magazines. From the beginning the work term fit like a custom-made leather glove allowing me to blend my past experience in security, psychology and customer service with my love of computers and technology. The work-term position quickly became a full-time Systems Administrator position, and today I help to maintain a network of more than 100 users and virtually anything that plugs into an outlet or takes batteries for Canada Wide. I am so glad that when it came time for me to make my decision at that fork in the road, I went with what suits me best. I love where it has taken me.

———

Here is another story from a member of the Canada Wide team. Beth McKenzie is an Account Manager for *BCBusiness* magazine.

About a year after moving here from the States, I reluctantly started to look for a job, knowing that I would never find a company as wonderful as my last, whom I was with for 10 years. Not being from the area, I had never heard of *BCBusiness* or Canada Wide Magazines when I came in for an interview.

I wasn't even 10 minutes into my interview (with VP of Sales Debbie McLean and Sales Manager Rebecca Legge) when I knew that Canada Wide was the place for me! Fortunately, they felt the same way, and after a few trips back to meet several people, I was offered the job. I started as an Account Manager for *BCBusiness* magazine three weeks later.

Toward the end of my first week here, my husband and I found out that we were going to have a new addition to the family. I was both excited and nervous about announcing the news to my new team, but being such a strong family-oriented company, everyone was very happy for me. During the several months that followed, I fell in love with my job, my team and my new home! In fact, so much so, that I returned to work only five months after starting my maternity leave.

I've been at Canada Wide now for just over two years. Every day I learn something new, every day I'm inspired by all the wonderful people I work with and every day I love my job!

———•—•———

A MASTER KNOWS: What you criticize, you drive out of your life. You become what you praise. Therefore, send letters of congratulations to those who have accomplished more than you.

———•—•———

An important part of focusing on your own talent is not being envious of what other people have accomplished. Geraldine Laybourne, who is Chairman and CEO of Oxygen Media, recalls a company policy that dealt with exactly that challenge.

"When I was at Nickelodeon," she says. "We had 10 commandments that we followed whenever we started a new business. To me, the most important one was 'Thou shalt not covet thy neighbour's wife, thy neighbour's donkey, or thy competitor's success.' This is especially true in television, where so many people just keep their eye on what the other networks are doing. They'll try to find the next *Desperate Housewives*, but the look-alikes never amount to a whole lot. I've done that a couple of times and fallen flat on my face. So I try not to get distracted by what worked for others. I always have an eye on the competition, but it's not to do what they're doing. It's to see where the holes are. I've built businesses by looking at conventional wisdom and going exactly the opposite way."

CHAPTER 18

"Today's mighty oak is simply yesterday's nut that held its ground."
— Unknown

Masterpiece Tool:
Exercise Self-Discipline

The most important habit you can develop for success, achievement and happiness in life is the habit of self-discipline. It is the ability to make yourself do what you should do, when you should do it, whether you feel like it or not. Self-discipline is the key to self-mastery and self-control, and that is why the happiest, most successful and most respected men and women in our society are men and women who have great self-discipline.

Even if you don't think that you possess it now, you can learn this habit with practice, and if you want to test just how important a skill it is, simply think of some public figure whom you admired and respected at one time for their accomplishment — then you found out that they had succumbed to a weakness, perhaps they covered up some misdoing within their organization or they didn't keep their word on an issue that was critical to an individual or group that they had power over — and remember how that lack of judgment diminished their character in your view.

These are moments of truth that we all encounter in our lives, moments when others let us down or when we let ourselves down.

It takes determination to learn self-discipline and I believe it begins with respect for your parents. I remember when I was young and went to boarding school in England. The train ride from Victoria Station to Heathfield was about two-and-a-half hours and my mother would put me on the train and give me a sandwich for the trip.

Like many of the other children on the train, I didn't always like what was in the sandwich I was given and often I didn't want to eat it. Once we pulled out of the station, many of them would throw their sandwiches out the window, but I could never bring myself to follow suit. Given the fact that my mother had taken the time to make the sandwich for me, I believed that out of respect for her, the least I could do was to eat it.

Looking back, I realize that it must have been very difficult for my mother to let me go and live away from home at such a young age (I started school, like all children in Great Britain, at age four), and sending me off with a sandwich was one way of showing that she loved me. It may sound funny, but even today with both of my parents having since passed away, I still gauge my life by the expectations that they had for me. They gave up so much to give me the opportunity to be successful and I will always owe them for it.

Last year I had the tremendous opportunity to work with the American company Auto-Owners Insurance, which is head-quartered in Lansing, Michigan. This is a Fortune 500 company that generates over $5 billion a year in revenue and is one of the largest insurers in the country. In offering me the opportunity to speak with 1,500 of their associates over a period of four days, company CEO Roger Looyenga explained that they had chosen me because I shared the same values as they do.

Following my time with the company, Looyenga relayed the message that everyone who attended my presentations was very impressed with the fact that I had done my homework in researching what Auto-Owners is all about.

"Your whole presentation really reinforced our values," Looyenga told me.

As a result of the eight presentations (each of them lasting two-and-a-half hours) that I did for Auto-Owners, they have invited me to present my message 24 more times over the next two years.

Here are the values that Auto-Owners keeps front and centre in everything they do:

Honesty — When the company sells a policy, they want their policyholder to know that the company will pay everything they promised to pay.

Hard Work — If associates want to advance at Auto-Owners, they are expected to show up on time, occasionally put in a few extra hours, be a good student by learning all they can and work hard with a positive attitude. The high value that is placed on self-motivation and hard work has been handed down from one generation of company leaders to the next, and from one generation of associates to the next.

Prudence — Although it is a Fortune 500 company, Auto-Owners doesn't own a corporate jet or allow associates to fly first class. The company also doesn't have a budget. Rather, any expense over a set limit (other than fixed costs like payroll or utilities) must be approved by the division officer or executive committee to ensure that the money is spent prudently.

Loyalty — The company shows loyalty to their associates by doing all they can to facilitate their success. On average, 60 per cent of an associate's income is matched with benefits. The company also has a policy to show loyalty to their agents who operate in small communities by not contracting with a competing agency (even if doing so might bring in more revenue).

The Team — Senior executives for Auto-Owners meet for

lunch five days a week. This enables them to share information and work better as a team. The company also provides associates with the opportunity to move from one department to another and learn different aspects of the business so that they can take on new challenges and be more effective members of the team.

Their Relationships — Auto-Owners values a healthy relationship with their associates and agents based on trust and open lines of communication.

Opportunity for Their Associates — The company is committed to finding out where an associate fits best so they can reach their potential. Just about anyone who is willing to work hard, give extra effort, serve the rest of the team and the customer, could make it to the top of the company.

The Customer — A commitment to customer service comes from the top down within Auto-Owners. That translates to serving not just the needs of policyholders, but also those of the agents who bring business into the company.

Stability and Consistency — Auto-Owners provides stability by developing leaders from within the company rather than importing them from outside. When you have executive officers who have spent 20 years or more with the company, they understand the culture and perpetuate it. This way you don't have a change of philosophy, vision and direction every time you have a change in leadership.

Profit — Auto-Owners values making profit for the company's stakeholders who are primarily the policyholders. However, it does not drive the company. If it did, the company would tend to cut staff and service in an effort to cut costs and increase profit.

In working with the people at Auto-Owners, what struck me most is just how important these values are to their agents and associates. By practising what they preach, they have built up a tremendous network of trustworthy and loyal people who are all focused on contributing to the company's success.

My advice to any business large or small is to post your values so everyone can know them, then live those values — from your senior management on down.

———·•·———

A MASTER KNOWS: It is important to cultivate only the habits that you are willing should master you.

———·•·———

Here are some tips that will help you build self-discipline:

Start with small things first. Learning to be self-disciplined in the little things in life prepares the way for bigger successes. Identify the main areas where you lack discipline and focus on these. They could include:

- Keeping your workspace tidy (find a home for each of the items you need and get rid of the rest);
- Getting up when the alarm goes off (reward yourself for getting up on time by playing some of your favourite music while you go about your morning routine);
- Returning telephone calls within 24 hours (set aside a half hour or so at the end of each workday to return calls; when someone leaves a message, at the very least they expect an acknowledgement);
- Arriving at work on time (try going into work 10 minutes early one day and see how it feels to walk into the office and sit down at your desk without feeling stressed — if it feels good, do it again the next day).

Choose one or two items to start working on and add new

items as the older ones become part of your regular routine. Before long, you'll be amazed at how much more time you seem to have and how much easier your day flows when you aren't constantly scrambling to keep up.

Get yourself organized. If you don't control your time, everything — and everyone — else will. Make a schedule and stick to it. Have a to-do list of things you need to accomplish and mark them off as you complete them. If you find yourself spending more than five or 10 minutes on something that isn't on your schedule or your list, redirect yourself and get back on schedule. Many business people find it helpful to carry a PDA device (to which all of their appointments and client information can be downloaded directly from their computer).

Finish what you start. Many people are good at starting projects, far fewer are as good at finishing them. If you're someone whose life is littered with unfinished projects, take heart. The best way to set yourself up for success with any new undertaking is to spend more time planning and assembling the resources you will need before you begin and enlist the help of others to provide encouragement and check in with your progress to keep you motivated.

Entertain yourself with active pursuits. When you have free time, do things that are active and productive instead of merely tuning out the world via the TV, video games or the computer. Read a good book, work on a hobby, plan an outing, have a conversation with someone, listen to music or take a walk. In other words, learn to entertain yourself with things that are stimulating, challenging and creative and these activities will repay you with a greater sense of connection and accomplishment.

Keep your word. When you make commitments, see them through. If you say you're going to do something, do it — when you said you would do it and how you said you would do it. An important part of practising this habit is developing the ability to properly evaluate whether you have the time and capability to do something before you commit to it. Live by the motto, "under-commit and over-deliver."

Tackle the most difficult tasks first. Most people do just the opposite; spending their time doing the easier, low-priority tasks. But when they run out of time and energy, the difficult, high-priority tasks still remain undone — and that's where we lose credibility with others. When you do the tough stuff first, you can relax and enjoy the easy tasks knowing that you have already taken care of business.

CHAPTER 19

"Living on Earth is expensive, but it does include a free trip around the sun every year."
— Unknown

Masterpiece Tool:
Choose to Be a Life-Long Optimist

One of the most powerful and uplifting mental habits that we can — and should — master in our lives, is that of being an optimist. After all, you become what you think about most of the time and that's why the healthiest, happiest, most successful and respected people in society are optimists. Optimism is the cornerstone of industriousness and dynamism because optimists think of what they want and how to get it most of the time. It motivates and stimulates them to perform at higher levels. And, best of all, it's contagious. Therefore, if you haven't yet got it, make a point of hanging around with optimistic people and you will soon catch it.

———

I graduated from Lester Pearson High School in New Westminster in 1959, when rock and roll was in its heyday with Elvis Presley, The Everly Brothers and Neil Sedaka, complete with sweater clubs, bobby socks, sock hops and hanging out at the local drive-in restaurant.

Although we were good kids (never malicious or disrespectful), we did like to push the envelope in regards to our relationship with our teachers and coaches. This included practical jokes and horsing around, but when they drew a line in the sand, we knew not to cross it.

I believe the relationship we had with our teachers and coaches was unique to that time, and looking back, I realize what a positive influence their mentorship has had on my life. Many of these men went on to become legendary names in British Columbia, names such as Ernie Nyhog (who was my homeroom teacher in grade 10, and my basketball coach), Bill Popowich (science teacher and soccer coach), Bill Kushner (football coach) and many others.

Thanks to Dave MacDonald, one of the best basketball players to come out of New Westminster (he and his brother Steve started Western Cablevision in New Westminster which they sold several years later to The Rogers Group), we have been able to stay in touch with these giants among men. For about 20 years now, Dave has hosted a luncheon every December at The Vancouver Club for students, teachers and coaches from those days.

In 2005, there were about 25 of us at the luncheon, and these days it's difficult to tell the difference between the teachers and the students. During the meal, I sat beside Stan Stewardson, who was once the head basketball coach at Simon Fraser University (one of his claims to fame is that he has been a student of the game for many, many years and arguably the winningest coach at SFU), and he reminded me how attitude and mental toughness over every-thing else wins games and makes good players great.

On my other side at the table was Bill Kushner, who is now 78 years old and still an active teacher at a private school in Delta. Bill played professional football for two years with the Calgary Stampeders and one year with the BC Lions of the Canadian Football League (CFL). When I asked him during the lunch, what it was that appealed to him about coaching, he told me that the main reason he had gone into coaching was to infuse everyone with a positive mental attitude.

"Attitude is everything in life," he told me.

I left the luncheon reminded of just how much these teachers made an impression on me as a young student and how they continue to remind me of the importance of a positive mental attitude in everything that I do.

"The ripple effect of a leader's enthusiasm and optimism is awesome. So is the impact of cynicism and pessimism. Leaders who whine and blame engender those same behaviours among their colleagues. I am not talking about stoically accepting organizational stupidity and performance incompetence with a 'What, me worry?' smile. I am talking about a gung-ho attitude that says 'we can change things here, we can achieve awesome goals, we can be the best.' Spare me the grim litany of the 'realist,' give me the unrealistic aspirations of the optimist any day."

— Colin Powell

Speaking of attitude, I am reminded of a recent taxi ride I took with my wife Kay in Las Vegas. We were on our way from the Mandalay Bay Hotel to the fashion mall, when Kay tried to strike up a conversation with the driver by asking him how his day was going.

"I'd rather be doing anything than driving this cab," the fellow grumbled in response.

Thinking that perhaps he had simply taken the job as a temporary measure to make ends meet or some such thing, Kay asked the driver how long he had been driving a cab.

"Thirty years," came the answer.

Kay and I looked at each other in amazement. Coincidentally, he had begun his career as a cab driver around the same that I started Canada Wide Magazines with one small TV listings magazine. I thought of all that I had accomplished in those 30 years and how my company had grown. I couldn't imagine sticking with something that I genuinely disliked doing for so long. Yet, judging by his hostile disposition and overall sour outlook, I got the impression that this cab driver had most likely been sharing his poor attitude with customers for many of those 30 years.

It's true that life doesn't always present us with the opportunities that we think we deserve. However, in my experience, the happiest and most successful people in the world are the ones who have an ability to find opportunity in the most unlikely places.

Imagine if this particular cab driver had shown up for his first day on the job 30 years ago with a positive attitude and a desire to be the best darn cab driver in Las Vegas. What if he had taken the time to learn as much as he could about the city so that he could be a knowledgeable guide for his passengers? What if he chose to smile as he opened the door for each new customer and helped them into the car before taking care of their luggage and then offering them a free map of local attractions? What if he had developed a reputation as the nicest, friendliest driver in the city and passengers began to ask for him by name . . . and what if, 30 years later he had built a company of his own with a fleet of 30 cars (one for each year he had been in business)? What if only he had believed in himself . . . what if?

I look at my own life 30 years after starting with one little magazine. Today, I enjoy great respect in the city where I live, high regard from other publishers, I have the loyalty and admiration of my colleagues and staff — and I look forward to each new day as an opportunity to do more. The best is yet to come because I am still working on my masterpiece.

———•+•———

A MASTER KNOWS: Having a positive mental attitude enables us to ask how something can be done, rather than saying it can't be done. Our attitudes and the choices we make today will be our life tomorrow, so we should choose them wisely.

———•+•———

Hollywood tour guide Stephen Schochet (who, by the way, loves his job and it shows) tells a funny story about the late actor, John Wayne, who was well known for his easygoing nature.

Schochet notes that for the last 30 years of his life, John Wayne often had a profound effect on people who crossed his path. Meeting him in person for some was like meeting Abraham Lincoln or George Washington. Yet the Duke usually stayed humble and almost always kept his sense of humour.

On one such occasion when he was out with a group of friends in a restaurant, the Duke excused himself to go to the men's room and when he came back his pant leg was wet.

"Hey Duke, what happened?" one of his friends asked.

"Nothing," replied John Wayne. "Happens all the time. I'm used to it."

"What happens?" the friend persisted.

The Duke, looking slightly annoyed, explained. "All right, if you must know, I'm standing in the men's room taking care of business and there's some yahoo standing right next to me and he says, 'Oh my god, you're John Wayne!' and suddenly he whirls around towards me . . ."

CHAPTER 20

*"Treat your customers like they own you,
because they do."*
— Mark Cuban

Masterpiece Tool:
Focus on Both Sales and Marketing

I remember one evening sitting in my hotel room at one of the Delta hotels, winding down after I had delivered a speech. As I sat there I started to notice all of the products and services that the hotel was offering to guests in addition to the accommodations, including:

- pay TV
- candies
- mini bar
- golf balls
- bath robes
- binoculars
- room service
- playing cards
- laundry services
- hair salon and spa services
- meeting rooms and business services

As I looked around the room at all the ways in which the hotel was anticipating the needs of their guests and then offering a range of products or services to fill those needs, I realized just how often we as business people overlook opportunities to serve our customers.

To be successful in business, we need to focus on both marketing and sales. With my own company, as we approached our 10-year anniversary and did a thorough review of our operations, it became quite clear that while we were very strong on the sales side, we hadn't paid the same attention to the marketing side of the equation.

Marketing and sales, while they have common elements, really serve different functions for your business. Marketing is all of the things that you do to build awareness of your product or services and your brand (it doesn't necessarily generate revenue). On the other side, sales activities generate income, but they don't necessarily build awareness of your brand in the marketplace.

How that translated to the bottom line for our 10-year-old company was that we put a lot of energy into making sales and we had been very successful in generating profit in certain markets. What we were lacking was an understanding from within the broader business market of what the company was all about and how, through our magazines, we could offer them exposure that could compete with or be superior to what they were getting from other media such as newspapers, radio and television. Realizing this, we understood the importance of having both a strong sales team and a great marketing strategy.

Why You Need to Put Sales Before Marketing

While I was in Calgary at a conference, I attended a seminar on negotiating skills. The speaker was a colleague from Calgary by the name of Tim Breithaupt, and he related a story about people's perceptions of sales and marketing. Tim told me about another convention that he was attending with an associate by the name of Peter Urs Bender. There were 300 delegates at this convention and

Tim and Peter each had a book available for sale. Tim's book was all about sales while Peter's was on marketing. By the end of the convention, Tim had sold just two books while Peter sold 300.

When I asked him for his opinion on this, Tim attributed it to the perception that many people have that marketing is quite a bit sexier than sales.

In my mind, those numbers should have been reversed and the reason for this is simple. Most often when companies fail, it is due to a lack of sales. The single most common reason for a lack of sales in a company that offers a viable product or service is poorly trained salespeople. Seventy per cent of salespeople who make sales calls never ask for the business. The reason they don't is because they are afraid of rejection. They are afraid of hearing the word "no." The five magic words in the world of sales are, "May I have your business?" If you don't train your salespeople to ask for the business, you won't have any revenue, period! Whether we like it or not, cash flow is king in the business world.

A MASTER KNOWS: The importance of knowing what your "sizzle" is (i.e., the thing that makes your company and your product or service special) and then either finding or creating opportunities to share that sizzle with the world.

I had the biggest single sale of my books in one session just recently following a presentation that I did for a group in Langley based on my book *The Runway of Life*. And it all came about from a sales technique that my daughter Rebecca learned from the people who run a business sales training company called Train the Trainer. The day before my presentation, I was sitting talking with my daughter and she told me how she had learned that rather than telling the customer, "You need to buy my product," a good salesperson lets the product sell itself.

Here's how she applied it to my book sales.

Throughout my presentation on *The Runway of Life*, I often refer to stories or passages from within the book (by referencing the notes I keep on the podium), without actually showing the book to the audience until the end of the presentation when I hold it up and say, "If you'd like to purchase a copy of *The Runway of Life*, please see me at the back of the room."

Rebecca instructed me to change the way I do my presentation. "Instead of referring to your notes, I want you to hold a copy of your book in your hand as if you had just been browsing through it. Then, when you refer to a story or passage, I want you to open the book to the page in question and read from it, saying something like, 'Right here in Chapter 7 is the story of how I ended up sharing a stage with two snake charmers . . .' or 'The list of my best networking tips starts on page 171 and here are a few of my favourites . . .' In this way, instead of giving them the hard sell, you are giving them a taste of your product that leaves them wanting more."

I followed the technique just as Rebecca had explained it to me, and I can tell you, the people in that audience were running to the back of the room before I had even finished speaking. I was both shocked and thrilled at what an amazing difference a little sales technique like that could instantaneously make in my sales. You can bet that I'm going to be following through to make sure that every member of Canada Wide's sales team has access to the training that Rebecca received.

Here are 12 tips to help you maximize your sales:

1. **Get the right education and training.** Invest your time in taking courses and reading books to help you acquire the knowledge you need to be effective in every selling situation. Education teaches you how to think. Training shows you how to apply that knowledge skillfully in real-life sales situations.

2. **Develop your selling savvy.** In his best-selling book, *How to Be a Great Sales Professional*, author Nido Qubein talks about the importance of developing "selling savvy" in five critical areas: (a) understanding the selling process so well that every aspect of it becomes second nature; (b) understanding people well enough to influence them to buy; (c) knowing how to use all your skills to get the sale; (d) developing street smarts, the instinctive intelligence that comes from watching and interacting with people; (e) and developing the discipline to consistently follow your sales strategy.

3. **Always deal with the decision-maker.** Make sure you are making your sales presentation to the person with the authority to make purchases and to influence repeat sales. If the person you are speaking to does not have this authority, you are wasting your time.

4. **Stay informed.** Keep pace with business developments in your community, the country and the world. Scan the business section in the local and national newspapers every day. Check out the day's business appointment announcements and scan the classified section to see who's hiring — often a tip-off that there may be growth or changes in a potential customer's company. Listen to the news on the radio while you are in transit, and watch television news on a variety of networks.

5. **Ask the right questions,** and then listen, listen, listen. Ask thoughtful questions about your customers' needs. If you listen carefully, most customers will tell you exactly what they want or need. They'll tell you how to sell them and will give you the information you need to help them solve the problem. Asking the right questions and cultivating good listening skills will go a long way toward winning your customers' confidence and loyalty. You're not learning anything when you're talking.

6. **Always ask for the order.** Your sale is not complete until you close the order. There are many approaches to closing, but ultimately you must learn to ask for the sale. Ask, "Should we proceed with this idea?" and then write up the order.

7. **Plan ahead.** Time is a priceless commodity — for you and your prospective customers. To make the most of every hour and maximize your sales potential, you need to plan your sales calls a minimum of one week in advance.

8. **Identify potential business.** Spend time analyzing where your sales increases will come from. They won't just happen. You need to search them out.

9. **Always have five new accounts in development.** Your client list is ever changing — a dynamic combination of long-time clients, new clients and clients who have moved on. It's critical that you always have an eye on new client development. Remember: He who sows sparingly will also reap sparingly and he who sows bountifully will also reap bountifully (2 Corinthians 9:6).

10. **Always carry an adequate supply of business cards.** Don't underestimate the importance of your business card, as it represents you to your client. It provides customers with

critical contact information and makes it easy for them to do business with you. Don't let a potential sale get past you because your client didn't know where to find you.

11. **Push yourself.** Motivation is what turns knowledge and skill into success. Work on it. Establish realistic goals to help guide your efforts.

12. **Revisit past customers.** Call customers you haven't seen for a while, including the ones who did not purchase your product. After all, business changes almost daily, and yesterday's no might be today's yes.

CHAPTER 21

*"People make a mistake who think my art
has come easily to me. Nobody has devoted so
much time and thought to composition as I.
There is not a famous master whose
music I have not studied over and over."*

—— Wolfgang Amadeus Mozart

Masterpiece Tool:
Be a Hard Worker

I was born in London, England, and grew up as an only child in a small town called Greenford just outside of London. As I've mentioned before, the local theatre was the major source of entertainment in those post-war years for people of all ages, and my mother would often take me to the movies. In those days, the seats were priced according to where they were located within the theatre.

The majority of seats on the main floor of the theatre were the sixpenny seats. These were the least expensive seats and there was always a huge lineup for them, which meant that you had to wait outside no matter what the weather was doing. The most expensive seats were called the 2/6's (which cost the equivalent of about 50 cents each). Besides the fact that they were the best seats in the theatre, just by paying a little more, you didn't have to wait outside in the sleet or snow.

If it was too hot, too cold, raining or snowing outside, my

mother would spoil me and we would sit in the 2/6's. Whenever we did, she made a point of telling that she did this so that I would know what it was like to have the very best that life had to offer (despite the fact that she had to sacrifice something else in order to pay for it). The lesson for me was that it was possible to obtain the finer things in life, but you had to be willing to work for them.

Here in North America, we are so fortunate that those things that are considered luxuries for most people in the world (a comfortable home, a nice car, a good education for our children) are readily available to anyone who is willing to work hard to obtain them.

———

A MASTER KNOWS: Happiness does not come from doing easy work but from the afterglow of satisfaction that comes after the achievement of a difficult task that demanded our best. The art is nothing without the gift, but the gift is nothing without the work.

———

AND THEN SOME . . .
These three little words are the secret to success.
They are the difference between average people and the top people in most companies. The top people always do what is expected, and then some . . .
They are thoughtful of others; they are considerate and kind, and then some . . .
They meet their obligations and responsibilities fairly and squarely, and then some . . .They are good friends and helpful neighbours, and then some . . .
They can be counted on in an emergency, and then some . . .
I am thankful for people like this, for they make the world more livable.

Their spirit of service is summed up in three little words . . .
AND THEN SOME.

——————

In North America, the **highest-paid** people (those who go after what they want in life) work on average a 60-hour week. The **longest-paid** people (those who are looking for a ride on the gravy train) work fewer than 25 hours per week.

In every study of successful people — athletes, executives, entrepreneurs or self-made millionaires in any field — the most obvious habit they all have in common is that they work much longer and harder than their co-workers or competitors.

If you do more than you are paid to do, sooner or later, you will be paid for more than you do. Unfortunately, this is not a widely accepted truism. In fact, many people take the opposite approach with an attitude like: "When they pay me what I'm worth, I'll give them what they pay for." The problem with this line of reasoning is that if you aren't willing to give something in order to get something, you never give anyone the opportunity to value your contribution.

In many ways, ours is a society based on instant gratification and entitlement, we want what we want, when we want it, whether we have earned it or not!

——————

"You will never possess what you are unwilling to pursue."
— Mike Murdock

——————

Ivan Seidenberg, the chairman and CEO of Verizon, relates how hard work paid off early in his career, "My first boss — he was the building superintendent and I was a janitor — watched me sweep floors and wash walls for almost a year before he mentioned that I could get tuition for college if I got a job with the phone company. When I asked him why he'd waited so long, he said, 'I wanted to see if you were worth it.'"

The message: Work hard, have high standards and stick to your values, because somebody's always watching.

———

"In theory, there is no difference between theory and practice.
But in practice, there is."

— Jan van de Snepscheut

CHAPTER 22

*"So let us begin anew — remembering on
both sides that civility is not a sign of weakness,
and sincerity is always subject to proof.
Let us never negotiate out of fear. But let us
never fear to negotiate."*

— John F. Kennedy

Masterpiece Tool:
Learn to Be a Negotiator

Whether or not it is an integral part of your job, being able to successfully negotiate with others is an important skill in life. After all, we all face situations where we must reach agreements with others and solve problems that involve people with different, or even conflicting, needs. Even if we don't call it by its name, negotiation is something that takes place daily in our lives — with family, friends, colleagues, customers — the list is virtually endless.

Although we all want to win, negotiation isn't just about getting your own way or giving in. In fact, these are the results when people fail to negotiate. If you won't, or can't, negotiate, then either you or the people around you are likely to end up feeling frustrated and resentful. And while someone may end up with the upper hand, it will be at the cost of a good working relationship.

What successful negotiation is about is allowing both sides to reach a good outcome, or at least one that they feel they have contributed to and can live with. Such an agreement will almost certainly involve compromise on both sides.

One of the most important factors to keep in mind when entering into a negotiation is that not everyone wants the same thing out of a deal. Take buying a car, for example. The dealer wants a sale and to make a profit. If sales are slow, they may have a cash-flow problem and be willing to settle for a lower price in order to generate cash. The customer, on the other hand, wants a vehicle. Factors that affect him, besides the cost, might include style, warranties, ease of maintenance, gas mileage, payment terms and other details that the dealer doesn't really care about. The art of negotiation is to find the common ground on which a deal can be made.

———————

Here is a story from a negotiator who kept listening until he learned how he could build a win-win solution.

While working with a group of real estate investors from a big city, the negotiator went to a nearby town to attempt to purchase an apartment building with 150 units. The owner of the property was an elderly gentleman who was very sharp in terms of mental faculties, but he appeared to be indecisive about the sale. The one thing he kept emphasizing was that he didn't want anyone in town to know that the apartment was for sale, a request with which the negotiator was eager to comply because he wasn't eager to have any competition for the purchase.

During several return trips, the negotiator talked at length with the old gentleman. Even more importantly, he listened to attempt to find the key to the puzzle. He tried to learn what the older gentleman's motives for selling were and what was holding him back from proceeding, so he could work with the first and find solutions to the second. He already knew that price was not a factor, as he was more than willing to pay the figure that had been named.

After some time, the negotiator learned that the building was being managed by the owner's son-in-law, who had never been able to keep a job. Part of the reason the family had built the apartments in the first place had been to provide a good job for the son-in-law. Unfortunately, he had shown no aptitude for the business (the apartments consistently lost money) and therefore the elderly gentleman was torn over selling, knowing that a new owner would not retain the son-in-law (and he would become unemployed).

Having learned of this situation, the negotiator offered an option for the son-in-law to stay on as a consultant for two years after the sale — for a generous fee. That was the key. The older gentleman was relieved, knowing that he wasn't pulling a job out from under his son-in-law. The son-in-law was happy to be a "consultant" to the "big city investors" and to have a good income with very little responsibility attached. From the negotiator's point of view, the cost of keeping the son-in-law (which was a tax-deductible expense) was reasonable in relationship to the total investment.

The end result was that everyone walked away feeling that they got what they wanted from the transaction.

———————

"In business, you don't get what you deserve,
you get what you negotiate."

— Chester Karrass

———————

In any negotiation, there are four basic elements at play: time, information, options and tactics.

1. Time — In any negotiation, the party with the most time has a distinct advantage in that they can wait out the other side to get a better deal. If you are under a tight deadline, you're going to feel the pressure while the other side is calm, collected and patient.

Consider again the example of buying a car. If your current car is running well and you're in no hurry, you will likely negotiate a better deal for yourself. On the other hand, if your car has just broken down and the mechanic says you will need expensive repairs very soon, you are under considerable pressure to find a replacement before your car dies, making you less likely to shop around and negotiate until you get the best deal you can.

This is why sales presentations for big-ticket or luxury purchases such as timeshares offer time-limited deals that you must act on "RIGHT NOW!" It is a sales tactic contrived to put the buyer in a time constraint.

According to Randy Shuttleworth, owner of The Training Company, based in Edmonton, 80 per cent of concessions are made within the last 20 per cent of the negotiation time.

2. **Information** — When it comes to negotiating, information is money. The more knowledgeable you are, the better the deal you will get. Imagine, for example that it is time to renew your mortgage. If you simply go into your bank and agree to their rate (thinking that because you are a good customer, they will take care of you), the bank has no incentive to give you a competitive rate. However, if you walk into the bank and say, "The bank down the street is offering the same mortgage at a percentage point lower and they're willing to give me a $500 cash rebate on top of that. What can you offer me?" chances are that they are going to sit up and take notice.

3. **Options** — Always keep your options open by having alternatives available just in case you are unable to reach an agreement. At the same time, within your negotiations, don't try to tackle too many issues at once; it is best to break the negotiations into segments and handle them one at a time. That way, if you reach consensus on a majority of separate issues — but are stuck on one or two — there is more incentive for both sides to push through rather than throw away the whole deal.

4. **Tactics** — How you choose to approach a negotiation and how you choose to conduct yourself throughout will have a significant effect on the way that the other side responds to your needs. Nobody wants to help a self-centred, argumentative jerk, but they do want to help someone they like and have rapport with. Even if the other side is not conducting themselves in a tactful manner, don't let their manner distract you. Keep focused on your goals and priorities.

Unfortunately, in our world today, many people interpret negotiation as being the skill of persuading other people to accept their point of view. When it is said of someone that they are a good negotiator, it usually means that they get the best of their opponents. Many trainers present techniques for succeeding in this manner, using methods such as intimidation to win. What they don't consider is that when a deal is struck to the advantage of one party and the detriment of the other, seeds of disagreement and retaliation are planted.

—–·–—

A MASTER KNOWS: A successful negotiator finds out what the needs of the other party are and tries to meet them without losing sight of his own goals.

———•·•———

All skilled negotiators have certain characteristics in common. First of all, they know what they want out of the deal before entering into negotiations. They are also perceptive and look for opportunities to create a win-win situation. In addition, they are good listeners (open to hearing what the other side is looking for and trying accommodate it). They identify key issues quickly, are patient, use creativity and seek common ground. Most of all, they have empathy for others and therefore are interested in making sure that everyone's needs are considered.

———•·•———

Steps to a Successful Negotiation

Choose to Meet Halfway

Set out to reach a win-win situation. Both sides should leave the negotiation feeling they've come away with something and are satisfied.

> *"The most important trip you may take in life is meeting people half way."*
>
> — Henry Boyle

Take Time to Prepare

This is the most important step in many negotiations. You want to be as thoroughly informed as possible about the value of the items you are negotiating — both in terms of their general value and what they are worth to the other side.

Know Your Bottom Line

In most negotiations, there is a point beyond which you do not want to go (i.e., when you will walk away and consider other alternatives). Decide in advance (but don't disclose) what really matters to you and what doesn't matter so much. That way, you'll know where you're willing to compromise and where you're not. You should also be aware that this may change with more information and new ideas.

Build Respect

When the other side feels that you respect him or her, defensiveness is reduced and sharing of useful information is increased — which can lead to an agreement. When people feel disrespect, they become more rigid and are likely to withhold important information. Always begin by saying something positive and appreciative to the person you're negotiating with. For instance, "I've noticed how hard you've been working on this deal," or "You really did a good job on that report outlining the alternatives to the proposal." It will increase the goodwill on both sides. If the other party is angry or hostile, refrain from getting drawn into a fight. Keep smiling and being pleasant and sooner or later they'll calm down.

> *"Never cut what you can untie."*
>
> — Joseph Joubert

Don't Attribute Your Motives to Other People

It is not unusual to go into a negotiation and assume that any other intelligent person is going to think and feel the same way we do. Wrong. In many cases, people are strongly influenced by emotional factors that we have no knowledge of; that is why an important part of negotiating is listening to find out what the other party really wants.

Ask Questions

Before stating a position or making proposals, it is very helpful to inquire about the other side's interests and concerns. This will help you understand what is important to the other side and may provide new ideas for mutual benefit. Ask clarifying questions to really understand the other side's concerns in this negotiation. This will also help you determine their approach to negotiations, win-lose or win-win, to enable you to make more realistic proposals.

Listen

And keep listening. It's vital to understand what the other person is truly saying and their point of view. To listen shows respect and good intentions, and will make the other person feel valued.

Employ Cautious Disclosure

It is fully appropriate and wise to start a negotiation without disclosing all of your information and your "bottom line." Give yourself room to maneuver. Make sure you have something to offer the other party, as well as something you want. If the other side is using a win-lose approach and you disclose too much too soon, you will lose all of your bargaining power. If the other side is using a win-win approach, then you can work together to explore all possible solutions. They will disclose more and more information and you can do the same to build trust and create better solutions.

Make a Proposal

It is customary and proper to ask for more at the start than you expect to receive in the final agreement. By proposing your ideal settlement, it lets the other side understand your needs and allows you to show good faith later on by revising your offer after hearing their response. It helps to make a new proposal, rather than to criticize the one the other side made. By brainstorming a list of options together without criticizing them, an agreement may emerge that no one had thought of before and which everyone can live with.

"My father told me, you must never try to make all the money that's in a deal. Let the other fellow make some money too, because if you have a reputation for always making all the money, you won't have many deals."

— J. Paul Getty

Develop Trust

People tend to be more generous toward those they like and trust. An attitude of friendliness and openness generally is more persuasive than an attitude of deception and manipulation. Being honest about the information you provide and showing interest in the other side's concerns can help.

Back Up Your Position

If necessary, let the other side know in detail how strong your point of view is — by showing them financial information, legal precedents or other strong data that backs up your position. If you believe the other party's assumptions are based on false information, you will need to re-educate them in a tactful manner.

Keep Your Options Open

If you don't get what you want, then resist the impulse to insult the other person or storm out. End the negotiation politely, and with a smile. That way you can always try again later.

"He who has learned to disagree without being disagreeable has discovered the most valuable secret of a diplomat."

— Robert Estabrook

Write It Down

Many potentially great agreements fall apart because everyone's memory of them was different. You should write down the details so that both parties understand the exact terms — who has agreed to do what, when and where.

CHAPTER 23

*"Don't flatter yourself that friendship
authorizes you to say disagreeable things
to your intimates. The nearer you
come into relation with a person, the more
necessary do tact and courtesy become."*

— Oliver Wendell Holmes

Masterpiece Tool:
Develop a Pleasing Personality

In the speaking world, as indeed in business and life, up to 20 per cent of people will not like you or respond to your individual personality. In some cases, you may be able to do something about this and in others you will not.

As an individual, the kind of personality you develop can be your greatest asset or greatest liability, for it embraces everything that you control: mind, body and soul. Your personality determines more than just how others see you; it also greatly affects the way that you experience life. It shapes the nature of your thoughts, your deeds, your relationships with others and your ability to define your place in the world. Therefore, it is essential that you develop a pleasing personality — pleasing to yourself and to others. Here are some factors that make up a pleasing personality:

- a positive mental attitude (PMA)
- tolerance

- alertness
- courtesy
- a fondness for people
- flexibility
- tactfulness
- personal magnetism
- a pleasant tone of voice
- control of facial expressions
- sportsmanship
- sincerity
- a sense of humour
- humility of the heart
- ability to smile
- enthusiasm
- control of temper and emotions
- patience

————•—•————

More often than not, how we choose to approach our very first interaction with another person sets the tone for how the relationship develops, as is evidenced in the following story about a city man who bought a farm.

On the first day that he arrived on his new farm, the city fellow went out to look at the fence around his property (which had been the source of much quarreling for the previous owner). As he walked around the perimeter, the neighbouring farmer suddenly appeared and said to him, "That fence is a full foot over on my side."

"No problem," said the new owner, "We will set the fence two feet over on my side."

"Oh, but that's more than I claim," stammered the surprised farmer.

"Never mind about that. I would much rather have peace with my neighbour than two feet of earth," said the man.

"That's surely fine of you, sir," replied the farmer, "But I couldn't let you do a thing like that. That fence will stay right where it is."

We all have the ability to make ourselves more pleasing to others, but this doesn't mean acting or being phony (people will simply see through that and be put off). Nor does it mean you have to compromise your ethics, morals or the standard of your company. What it does mean is that you should endeavour to take a genuine interest in other people and approach your interactions with them in a sincere way by being interested in who they are and what they do.

My assistant at Canada Wide, Dale Clarke, has a story about how one such person's positive attitude and pleasing personality influenced her life and the career path that eventually led her to our company.

Earlier in my career, I spent several years working for Richmond Savings Credit Union. When I started with the company in 1993, the President and CEO was Kirk Lawrie. Kirk was a kind, caring and thoughtful person. He made it a priority to know his staff, all 400-plus of them. Kirk was an early-morning person (as was I) and I would often hear his whistle as he walked down the halls before 7 a.m. looking to see who else was in the building at that time of the morning and wanting to chat.

Throughout the years that I worked with Kirk, Richmond Savings subscribed to *BCBusiness* magazine, and members of the organization, usually the management and sales staff, often attended *BCBusiness* breakfast seminars. It was the spring of 1997, when I received an invitation from Kirk to attend a breakfast where Peter Legge was scheduled to speak. I was honoured to receive such an invite and readily accepted.

From the moment that he stepped up to the podium that morning, Peter captured the audience with his sense of humour, stories from his own life and a positive message that stuck with me for a long time afterwards. He talked with great respect of his parents and growing up as an only child. This in particular struck home for me, as I had a one-year-old son of my own at home. It was both comforting and inspiring to hear Peter speak of his childhood, his ambition, his goals, success and happiness. I was grateful to Kirk for inviting me to hear Peter speak and in the months that followed, I often thought of Peter's words.

On September 5, 1997, Kirk Lawrie passed away suddenly following a heart attack. I took this loss very hard, for not only was Kirk a well-respected leader with a wonderful sense of humour and a very caring way with his staff, he was also a role model and I had the greatest respect for him.

It's not surprising then, that for the next several years, I found myself with no particular direction. Try as I might, I couldn't find an organization where I had the same level of respect and admiration for the leader as I did for Kirk. For me, working for him had set the bar very high.

Then, in November 2004, I received a call from an associate who told me that Canada Wide Magazines was looking for an Executive Assistant. I knew this was the company that Peter Legge had started and I was excited about the opportunity. Could this be the position I had been waiting for?

If anyone had told me in 1997 that I would be working at

Canada Wide within the next 10 years, I wouldn't have believed it. I can still see Peter on stage at that breakfast seminar I attended with Kirk Lawrie. I've had the opportunity to see Peter speak several times now and whenever I do, I look around at the other men and women in the audience. I can see from their attentive looks and smiles of appreciation that his words have the same effect on them as they do on me. Because of his positive message and engaging delivery, Peter has a unique ability to help people to change the direction of their lives.

As Peter's assistant, I am grateful for the support and encouragement he has shown me, and for the chance it has given me to realize my full potential, day after day.

———

A MASTER KNOWS: The best way to sell yourself to others is first to sell the others to yourself. Check your attitude against this list of obstacles to a pleasing personality: interrupting others; sarcasm; vanity; being a poor listener; insincere flattery; finding fault; challenging others without good cause; giving unsolicited advice; complaining; maintaining an attitude of superiority; envy of others' success.

———

Although the way you treat others affects the way they treat you, the way another person treats you shouldn't determine the way you treat that person. Therefore, respond to what appears to you to be rude behaviour with the utmost kindness. You can't know what has gone on in that person's life that day, but you can assume that his or her day hasn't gone well — perhaps they are not feeling well, there is a difficulty at home or they feel under-appreciated and put upon by others. Whatever the cause of the rudeness, you don't have to accentuate the problem. A kind word or a gentle, understanding smile may be just what they need to remind them that everyone is not against them. Even if it doesn't work, you can walk away from the interaction knowing that you didn't add fuel to the fire.

William James once said, "The deepest principle in human nature is the craving to be appreciated." And probably the most important rule in the world is, "Do unto others as you would have them do unto you."

Imagine a sign hanging around every person's neck that only you can read, and it says, "Make me feel important." One of the easiest things you can do to accomplish this is to let people know that you are never too busy to follow up on the small things — like returning phone calls and emails promptly, acknowledging an invitation, a kindness or a gift by sending a card or note and by offering congratulations when they are due.

There's no doubt that criticism is easy to give but hard to take. Remember this the next time that you plan to hand some out and think about whether the goal you wish to accomplish — improving performance, quality of service or reducing errors — couldn't be achieved just as easily by focusing on the positive.

Here is a story on that subject that you might enjoy.

A wise old gentleman retired and purchased a modest home near a junior high school. He spent the first few weeks of his retirement in peace and contentment . . . and then a new school year began. The very next afternoon three young boys, full of youthful after-school enthusiasm, came down his street beating merrily on every trash can they encountered. The crashing percussion continued day after day until finally the wise old man decided it was time to take some action.

The next afternoon, he walked out to meet the young percussionists as they banged their way down the street. Stopping them, he said, "You kids are a lot of fun. I like to see you express your exuberance like that; I used to do the same thing when I was your age. Will you do me a favour? I'll give you each a dollar if you'll promise to come around every day and do your thing." The kids were elated by the prospect of getting money to beat on the garbage cans and continued to do a bang-up job. However, after a few more days, the old-timer greeted the kids again, but this time he had a sad smile on his face. "This recession's really putting a big dent in my income," he told them. "From now on, I'll only be able to pay you 50 cents to beat on the cans." The noisemakers were obviously displeased, but they accepted his offer and continued their afternoon ruckus.

A few days later, the wily retiree approached them yet again as they drummed their way down the street. "Look," he said, "I haven't received my Social Security cheque yet, so I'm not going to be able to give you more than 25 cents from now on. Will that be okay?"

"A lousy quarter?" the drum leader exclaimed. "If you think we're going to waste our time beating these cans around for a quarter, you're nuts! No way, mister. We quit!"

From then on, the old man enjoyed peace and serenity for the rest of his days.

In my personal experience of 30-plus years in business, when you criticize, people build up resistance and resentment. On the other hand, when you encourage people and build them up, you could literally ask them to perform the impossible and they will rise to the challenge and do all that they can not to let you down.

The same holds true with customers. If they like you and feel appreciated, people will find a way to do business with you — by

referring their friends, colleague and associates to your business —
even if they don't need what you are selling. On the other side of
the coin, if they don't like your attitude or your manners — even if
you offer exactly the product or service they require — they will
find a way **not** to do business with you.

Here are some ideas on ways to develop a pleasing personality:

1. *The greatest way to make a positive first impression is to
   demonstrate immediately that the other person — not you
   — is the centre of action and conversation.* Try to keep all
   of the attention for yourself and you'll miss opportunities
   for friendships, jobs, love relationships, networking and
   sales. Show that you are other-centred, and others will be
   drawn to the warmth of your generous personality.

2. *Use the name of a new acquaintance frequently.* "Janet, I
   like that suggestion." "Your trip to Asia must have been
   exciting, Andrew." By doing this you show not only that
   you have paid attention from the start (catching their name
   during introductions), equally as important, you'll make
   conversations more personal and be able to establish rapport
   more quickly.

3. *Demonstrate good listening skills.* In conversation, when
   the other person is speaking, give positive verbal cues with
   phrases like, "Hmmm . . . interesting!" "Tell me more,
   please" or "What did you do next?" Just as actors benefit
   from prompts, your conversational partner will welcome
   your assistance in keeping the exchange going. You can also
   show that you're a skilled listener with nonverbal actions
   such as maintaining steady eye contact. Remember how
   you've felt at a social event, when the person you are

speaking to appears to be looking over your shoulder, supposedly scoping out the next person he wants to corner.

4. *Speaking style impacts the impression we make on others.* Listeners judge our intelligence, education, cultural level and even leadership ability by the words we select and how we say them. Therefore, make sure you speak loud enough so you're easily heard, enunciate clearly, use words that are appropriate to the situation (street slang and cursing are not suitable in a business setting) and most importantly show your enthusiasm both in your voice and your facial expressions.

5. *Be careful what you say about others.* An offhand comment might be repeated and you'll soon be at the centre of a controversy. Don't waste your energy on gossip and remember that whatever you say about someone else is going to be interpreted by the person hearing it.

6. *Remember who you are.* Most of us more or less live up — or down — to our stereotypes. Compared to most of the world, North Americans are abrupt and action-oriented, we'd rather skip the small talk and get right down to business. This can be interpreted as rudeness by other cultures. Self-awareness (what we are as well as what we're perceived to be) can help us check our own behaviour and attend to the sensitivities of others.

7. *Employ humour, but proceed with care.* Although a quip or two might serve as an icebreaker, stay away from sarcastic remarks that could backfire, especially when meeting and establishing rapport with new people. Because you don't know a new acquaintance's sensitivities, prolonged joking might establish barriers that can't be overcome. The key is to be thoughtful about the kinds of witty remarks you make

or the jokes you tell. Make sure they are wholesome and appropriate to the audience to ensure that you do not give offence.

8. *Don't share the email addresses of business associates* (it is a breach of their privacy) or other contacts without their permission and don't be one of those people who constantly forwards jokes to everyone in their email address book unless you are specifically asked to share. Most people find it a nuisance to have their inbox clogged up with junk.

CHAPTER 24

*"I realized that they had already taken
everything from me except my mind and my heart.
Those they could not take without my
permission. I decided not to give them away . . .
And neither should you."*

— Nelson Mandela

Masterpiece Tool:
Build Strength Through Adversity

Adversity reveals true character. This was noted by the 14th-century mystic Thomas Kempis, who said, "Adversities do not make a man frail, they show what sort of man he is."

Oliver Wendell Holmes noted, "If I had a formula for bypassing trouble, I would not pass it round. Trouble creates a capacity to handle it. I don't embrace trouble; that's as bad as treating it as an enemy. But I do say meet it as a friend, for you'll see a lot of it and had better be on speaking terms with it."

It has often been said that experience is the toughest teacher because she gives the test first, and then the lesson. Those who face personal trials either rise to the occasion or fall down in despair. A crisis strips away all pretence, revealing true character and it is up to each one of us to choose whether we will be beaten down by the problems in our life or "use the difficulty" and build strength of character.

Following is a story from Canada Wide's Cathy Mullaly, now the Art Director of *BCBusiness*, about how she found the strength she needed to make it through a difficult transition.

I cried all the way home after my first day at Canada Wide Magazines. It was 15 years ago and I was just returning to the workforce following a maternity leave. I had quit a job that I truly loved — as an assistant art director with a monthly city magazine — a year earlier when I realized that after just 16 weeks (that's how long maternity leave was at that time) at home with a new baby and a very busy two-and-a-half-year-old, there was no way that I could manage working full time.

Having gotten things under control at home, I was looking forward to getting back to work after a year off and applied for a job as Art Director at Canada Wide Magazines. My interview was held in the boardroom and before I even had time to return home, I received a call saying that I had the job.

When I showed up for my first day of work, the company's offices were under renovation. I didn't remember it looking quite so glum, I thought to myself as I stepped into the reception area. Wires were hanging down, walls had gaping holes and construction workers wandered in and out. Corinne Smith met me at the front reception and as I looked apprehensively around she said to me, "Don't worry, we're just renovating. Everything is going to be fine."

She took me down the hallway to my "office," although it didn't look like much of an office at the time. Because of the renovations, the entire production department had been moved to a temporary location and people were practically sitting on top of one another. As I got my bearings, Corinne set me up with schedules. I was to be responsible for seven magazines, each of which published from four to six issues per year. I started my job on December 10 and within days, every one of the seven magazines went into production for their next issue — and they were all due by January 15!

What a shock. I had come from a monthly magazine, meaning we produced just one magazine per month. How on earth was I going to cope with seven different magazines in the same amount of time with only one assistant? I remember that Corinne was so calm as she listened to my concerns. "Don't worry," she said, "there's lots of help. You can do it, Cathy!" I spent the rest of the day in a bit of a daze trying to figure out how this would ever work and I cried all the way home.

It did indeed all work out, just as Corinne had said. The renovations were soon completed and I ended up with a great work space. All seven magazines managed to get finished and after 15 years in the job I would estimate that I have completed at least another 250 issues since then. I've also been through two more renovations, worked with some of the best people in the world and I'm very proud of the job I do.

I'm not saying that was the last time a few tears were shed because it wasn't. But looking back, there have been a lot more laughter and good times with a great team of people. Still, magazine publishing is a business of deadlines and challenges and I have faced many over the years. Thankfully, whenever those challenges have come my way, Corinne has always been there to say, "Don't worry, Cath! You can do it!" And I know I can.

———+·+———

"When you run out of red, use blue!"
— Pablo Picasso

———+·+———

A MASTER KNOWS: We only grow when we face the challenges of life head on, not by running away.

In the summer of 2001, I made a commitment to my youngest daughter Amanda that I would be a speaker at a teachers' conference she was helping to organize for three or four hundred of her colleagues in September. I was looking forward to the event, seeing it as a great opportunity to show her how proud I am of her work as a teacher. Then, just a few weeks before I was scheduled to speak, I suffered the serious stroke that I mentioned previously in this book.

While I was recovering, Amanda came to me and said, "Don't worry, Dad, you don't have to come and speak at the conference."

"There is no way that I am going to miss that conference," I told her determinedly. "I don't know how right now, but I will be there and I will give my presentation."

Not being able to drive myself, on the day of the conference I arranged for a limousine to pick me up at home and drive me to the school. Amanda met me at the curb and helped me inside where she showed me to a private waiting room. I appreciated the few minutes of time alone to gather my courage, given the fact that the stroke had distorted my facial features and I was feeling more than a little self-conscious as a result.

When it was time for me to speak, Amanda came to escort me to the stage. One side of my body was nearly lifeless, and she literally had to hold me up and help me onto the stage where I clung to the side of the podium for 40 minutes as I spoke. Following my remarks, I was touched to receive a standing ovation from the teachers, and Amanda helped me back down to my seat. During the coffee break a short time later, she helped me back outside to the limo and I went home and straight to bed.

Sometimes, after I have spoken to a group, people will come up to me and comment that I make what I do on the stage look so easy. I can tell you for a fact that day certainly wasn't easy for me, but it was important and the reward that I got in the end was worth any amount of struggle on my part. The very next week, I received the following card.

Dear Dad,

I am so proud and honoured that you were a part of our school conference. With daring and courage you came to our conference knowing you were not 100 per cent, but also knowing that you were not going to let me down.

I hope you know that had you not been able to speak, I would have been as proud of you as I am today. I am honoured that you gathered all your strength and talent for me.

You have often told the story of how you chartered a jet to get home for my graduation ceremony, doing whatever it took to keep your word. I think because I was younger I couldn't truly appreciate the lengths you were willing to go to make our family and me a priority.

Today, as an adult, I have experienced first hand what courage it took for you to speak at our conference and I know what this means.

I thank you — not only for speaking, but more importantly, for making me feel like the most important person in the world to you, as you so often do, and once again for modelling courage, commitment and dedication.

I love you,

Amanda

xxxooo

———•◦•———

"There's something bad in everything good and there's something good in everything bad."
— Michael Lewis (author of *Liar's Poker*)

———•◦•———

How you deal with the tough times really defines your character and tells the whole world who you truly are. Following is a list of some people who overcame great adversity to create their own masterpiece. I've printed this list in a previous book, but I think repeating these names will serve as a valuable reminder to us all.

Sarah Bernhardt was the most famous actress in France in the 19th century, and even after her leg was amputated in 1915 following a serious knee injury, she continued her career undiscouraged.

Marlee Matlin lost her hearing at 18 months of age but went on to win an Oscar for her debut role in the film *Children of a Lesser God*.

Woodrow Wilson had a learning disability but still served as President of the United States from 1913 to 1921.

Francisco Goya, the celebrated Spanish painter, became permanently deaf at the age of 45 and yet went on to create some of his most powerful work.

Albert Einstein is heralded as a scientific genius in spite of rumours that he suffered from a learning disability.

Ludwig van Beethoven, the famous composer, had become deaf by the time he created his magnificent *Ninth Symphony*.

John Milton had turned completely blind by age 43 but went on to write his most famous epic poem, *Paradise Lost*.

Thomas Edison had a learning disability but his inventions have significantly changed the world.

Harriet Tubman, a leader in the Underground Railroad, had narcolepsy but is celebrated as a heroine for her work in helping to abolish slavery.

A MASTER KNOWS: The secret of success of every man who has been successful lies in the fact that he formed the habit of doings things that failures don't like to do.

"We are all in the gutter, but some of us are looking at the stars."
— Oscar Wilde

CHAPTER 25

*"When you come to the edge of all the light
you have, and must take a step into the
darkness of the unknown, believe that one of
two things will happen to you: either
there will be something solid for you to stand
on, or you will be taught how to fly."*

— Patrick Overton

Masterpiece Tool:
Believe in Yourself

The famous American painter Georgia O'Keeffe knew when she was 12 years old that she wanted to be an artist. Although as an abstract artist, she realized she was somewhat ahead of her time, noting that, "I have things in my head that are not like what anyone has taught me — shapes and ideas so near to me — so natural to my way of being and thinking that it hasn't occurred to me to put them down."

Even though she showed natural talent from a young age and took a number of painting classes, O'Keeffe initially chose to pursue a more conventional career as an art teacher rather than a painter. It wasn't until a friend showed her work to an influential gallery owner in New York and he arranged an exhibition introducing her as a major young talent, that O'Keeffe was persuaded to give up teaching and become a professional artist.

About her famously vivid paintings of flowers, O'Keeffe once said, "I found I could say things with colour and shapes that I couldn't say any other way — things I had no words for."

O'Keeffe had a long and productive career, exhibiting more than 900 works of art during her lifetime. She continued to create art until her death in 1986 at the age of 98. Her advice to another artist, Russell Vernon Hunter, in many ways sums up the sense of wonder that she was able to portray through her work: "Try to paint your world as though you are the first man looking at it . . . the wind and the light and the cold . . . the dust and the vast starlit night."

"You cannot teach a man anything; you can only help him find it within himself."

— Galileo

While my daughter Amanda was finishing high school at Pacific Academy, she needed to earn a few dollars and decided to apply for a job as a retail clerk at Please Mum located in Lougheed Mall. At that time she was already seriously considering a career in teaching and felt it might be good experience to deal with moms and their children. Please Mum is a children's clothing store considered one of the best in the Lower Mainland.

After consulting us about her plans, Amanda went ahead and made an appointment for 10 a.m. one Thursday to be interviewed by the store manager. Her mother and I encouraged her to be on time, be polite and courteous, be aware of what was happening around her, dress smartly and just be herself. She arrived at the store at 9:55 a.m. and just as it was time for her interview to begin, the store suddenly began to fill up with customers. The store manager asked Amanda to delay the interview until she had attended to all the customers in the store.

The store was in fact swamped and the clerks on duty couldn't handle this sudden overflow of people. Without being asked, Amanda recognized the need and immediately became aware of what was happening around her and she began to serve the customers. She didn't ring up any of the items, but she had little piles of clothes on the counter, the right sizes, the right colours, the right fabrics, so that at the appropriate time all the sales manager needed to do was ring up the sales.

At about 11 a.m., the store began to empty out and the store manager turned to Amanda and said, "You've demonstrated exactly the kind of initiative that we are looking for. An interview is really not necessary. When would you like to start?"

———•+•———

A MASTER KNOWS: Experience is something you don't get until just after you need it, so you have to go with what you've got.

———•+•———

Canada Wide's own Jocelyn Snelling, our Credit Manager, tells a story about how the wrong job gave her just the motivation she needed to find the right one.

I was working at a job for only three weeks when I knew I was in the wrong company. As a result, every time Sunday night came around, I would feel slightly ill at the thought of having to go to work on Monday morning. My boyfriend at the time, bless his heart, got tired of listening to me gripe about the people I had to work with and literally said to me, "$#!*, or get off the pot, go look for another job." So I did.

Because I was already working at a brand new job, I couldn't really afford to take time off to go to interviews so I had to schedule them for after work hours. Therefore, I went for my first interview at Canada Wide Magazines at 5:30 p.m. Unfortunately, when I arrived at the front of the building, the lobby doors were locked! Not to be deterred, I ran around the building looking for any open doors, and fortunately, I found one open around at the back and made it just on time.

The interview with Heather Parker, now the Senior VP of Finance and Operations, went well, I thought and I left the building thinking, "This is exactly the job I want, but I probably won't get it." I was pleasantly surprised to get a callback interview with VP Karen Foss, which also went very well and I was hired. I later learned that a CGA and a lawyer were among the other candidates who had applied for the position and I often marvel at the fact that Heather and Karen decided to take a chance on a very young, inexperienced person like me. It's hard to believe that was 18 years ago.

———•—•———

Unfortunately, there are a great many people in this world who never realize their own true worth — and worthiness of success. It is very likely that no artist suffered more to bring his masterpieces into the world than Vincent van Gogh, whose struggle with mental anguish and bouts of depression are the things of which legends are wrought. And yet, few artists have ever lived life so intensely or left behind such a glorious legacy of their talent.

It has been noted that van Gogh created all of his more than 900 paintings within a 10-year period (he took his own life at the still-young age of 37) using a technique that grew more and more impassioned in its brushstroke, intense use of colour and movement of form and line.

Despite the fact that he lacked confidence in himself and sold just one painting during his lifetime, van Gogh's work is much coveted by modern collectors and museums — three of his paintings, *Sunflowers*, *Irises* and most recently *Portrait of Dr. Paul Gachet* (which went to a Japanese buyer in 1990 for $82.5 million), have, at different times, set record prices at auction.

Believe in Yourself

We all have moments of doubt in our life; it is how we handle those moments that determines our success. Understand and appreciate what you have achieved. Reflect. Think of the risks you have taken and the obstacles that you've overcome. Think about the difficult times and then look at where you are right now and how far you've come. Take a moment to tell yourself:

- I am capable.
- I can do this.
- I can make it happen.
- I can be successful.

"My breakthrough came very late in life, really only starting when I was 50 years old. But at that time I felt as though I had the strength for new deeds and ideas."
— Edvard Munch

CHAPTER 26

*"Efficiency is doing things right. Effectiveness
is doing the right things. Success is doing
the right things right, right now."*

— Nisandeh Neta

Masterpiece Tool:
Realize That Success (or Failure) is
All in Your Head

When we were just starting out with *TV Week*, we bought all of our editorial content from the King Syndicate in New York. One day the editor came to me and said, "I've got a big problem. We go to press at noon on Thursday and the horoscope column hasn't come in. What do I do?"

As is often the case at moments like this one, the first thought that popped into my mind was something that my dad always told me, "Be resourceful, be creative and do what is required." So I said to Linda, "Go into your office and write your own."

"What exactly do you mean by that?" she asked me.

"Well," I said. "It seems to me that our readers are expecting a horoscope in their issue of *TV Week* and many of them will be disappointed if they don't find one. So I am asking you to make it up. Just make sure that everyone has a good week next week."

So she did and I believe that thousands of our readers had the best week of the year even though they had no idea where it came from.

While this may be an amusing story, I think it also has a very serious point: We should be very discerning about what we allow to influence our lives if we are to create our masterpiece in life.

———•—•———

I've often heard the statistic that much of North America's wealth is in the hands of 50 people. When you consider that there are more than half a billion people living on the continent, it's a truly mind-boggling bit of trivia. However, in thinking about it, I would bet that if every one of those people went broke tomorrow, in 50 years they would have it all back again. The reason I say this is because in most cases, what made them rich in the first place is not what's in their pockets or their bank accounts; rather, it is what they carry around in their head. They possess what is called a "prosperous mindset" and we could all learn something from that.

Nido Qubein, President of High Point University, was born in Lebanon. He came to North America with less than $50 in his pocket and unable to speak a word of English. His mother told him, "Nido, if you want to be successful in America, you've got to walk hand in hand with those men and women who are infinitely more successful than you."

Nido set about learning English by focusing on a word a day, every single day. He also set about learning from the habits of very successful people, including the habit of developing a prosperous mindset. Today, he is considered to be one of the most successful professional speakers in North America and one of the most successful business people as well. In 2005, he was unanimously elected as the president of High Point University.

It's been said, "You can't have everything," or as I like to say, "You can't marry all of the girls," and that's basically true. You can't get every piece of business and you can't have all of the money (not that you need it all anyway). However, if you don't show up, if you don't have a willingness and a drive to succeed . . . if you don't even try, in the end you can expect to get exactly what you deserve: nothing!

Eighty per cent of our success in life can be attributed to showing up. If we want to be more successful, we need to show up and we also need to be willing to do the things that failures don't like to do. We need to use our creativity and imagination to look for ways in which we can be of benefit to others and then make our products or services indispensable.

Success breeds success.

If we want to learn what it takes to be successful, we should follow Nido's example by associating with and studying those who are more successful than we are so that we can learn from them and take the very best of what they are doing and apply it to our own life and career.

Of course, this includes developing that all-important prosperous mindset. A necessary part of a prosperous mindset is taking control of your finances and learning to live within your means — spending less than you earn each month. This is a habit that distinguishes those who respect how money can work for them from those who are constantly chasing after it and cursing the fact that they never have enough of it. Saving 10 per cent of all that you earn (which provides a sense of security and gives you something to invest for the future) also helps to develop a prosperous mindset, as does giving away 10 per cent — for the simple fact that it reinforces the belief that there will always be more.

*"When I chased after money I never had enough.
When I got my life on purpose and focused on giving of myself
and everything that arrived into my life, then I was prosperous."*
— Wayne Dyer

For more than 18 years I have been putting together a weekly insight for all Canada Wide staff that is both motivational and inspirational. Each week, I prepare a message for the following week and my assistant distributes them on Friday afternoon just before she leaves for the weekend. A copy of the insight is printed and placed on the desk of each staff member so that it is the first thing they see when they come into the office on Monday morning.

Each time over the years that I have contemplated stopping the insights, my staff have encouraged me to continue, saying that they look forward to reading them each week. It is a means of regular communication that has helped to bring us closer together as a company, as many staff members will send me an email or stop by my office to tell me how a particular insight affected them. One staff member who has been with me for nine years has even collected and saved every issue.

Over the years, other companies have also heard about my weekly insights and requested a copy to pass on to their own staff and customers. Today, I post the insights on my web site and literally hundreds of companies subscribe on a weekly basis. This is a free service that I provide because it is important to me and I hope that it helps bring other companies together as it has for us at Canada Wide.

Here's a story from Terri Mason, a member of the Canada

Wide Accounting department about how one opportunity changed her thinking about her own luck.

As the old saying goes, "Often it's not what you know, it's who you know." I have to confess that I've always been a little envious of people who get things because of who they know . . . until it happened to me.

Back in 1989, I found myself unemployed after leaving a job in retail that just hadn't worked out to be what I had been promised. On top of that, in order to take the job, I had moved to Calgary and away from my family.

So there I was, on my own and out of work, but try as I might I just couldn't figure out what I wanted to do. Without any real direction, I did a few odd jobs until the fall when my sister, who did accounts payable at Canada Wide, notified me that she was in need of some help. Despite the fact that I had no real working knowledge of accounting, I came in to help my sister out and while I was here her boss Heather Parker saw something that she liked in me.

Before long, I was offered a part-time position in the circulation department to help with Christmas promotions. This temporary job led to a full-time position due to growth in the company, and before I knew it, I had a career of my own.

Peter always says that you can have many careers in one place and I'm happy to report that after five years in circulation I went back into the accounting department to do the job I had come in to assist with originally.

Our company gives a watch to 10-year employees because they don't believe you should have to wait until you retire to get a gold watch. When I got mine in December of 1999, my very first thought was, "Not bad when you consider I never applied to work here."

———•+•———

A MASTER KNOWS: You weren't born to be average. You were created to excel. You have within you the seeds of greatness, filled with possibilities, incredible potential, creative ideas and dreams. You have been given insight, talent and wisdom. Now it is up to you to act on what you already possess.

If one dream dies, dream another dream, don't settle for mediocrity. Stop eating cheese and crackers. Instead, step into the banquet hall and hang around with the successful people — you never know what might happen as a result . . .

———•+•———

Consider this story about an idea that just wouldn't go away.

In the late fall of 1985, I was holidaying with my family and we were discussing how thrilled I was to be a part of Ray Addington's team on the British Pavilion, but I wished I could do more for Expo 86 because it would only come around once in my lifetime in Vancouver.

At the time, we were literally sitting on the beach at the Turtle Bay Hilton on the north end of the big island of Oahu when my wife suddenly turned to me and said, in response to my question:

"What kind of business are you in, Peter?"

"The magazine business," I answered, feeling somewhat as if I were being gently led by the hand, not unlike a small child.

"That's right, and who exactly is scheduled to open Expo 86?" she asked.

"Why, Prince Charles and Princess Diana," I replied.

"That's right," she said. "So why don't you make a special magazine commemorating their 10-day stay in Vancouver to open this world event?"

"That's it!" I exclaimed. "What a great idea!"

The original plan for the royals was that the Prince and Princess were going to be visiting Vancouver and Victoria for 10 days with the major focus of their visit being the opening of Expo 86. Our idea was to hire a few photographers and get the press credentials needed to follow them around to as many events as we could get into from the start to finish of their trip, and then produce a high-end souvenir magazine. The content for the magazine would be written, produced and printed within two weeks of their departure and the magazines would be for sale at every Commonwealth pavilion within Expo 86 for the duration of the fair, as well as at other distributors for a cover price of $9.95.

I came back to Vancouver very excited and presented the concept to both my finance and production teams. The finance people essentially told me, "Peter, it's the stupidest idea you've ever come up with."

Here is a list of their objections:

- We didn't have the photographers.
- We didn't have anyone lined up to write it.
- Who would print it on such short notice?
- We didn't have any press credentials.
- The logistics of putting it all together would be completely overwhelming.

Not to make matters worse, but I had also decided that we should pre-sell the publication by promoting it in our magazines. Of course, there was one small problem with that. We had absolutely no pictures of Charles and Diana to use for the promotion. I decided that I would have to fly to London to get some pictures (this was long before the Internet and other such modern facilities made it possible to have them sent electronically).

So I went over to London to visit the organization that

distributes officially sanctioned images of the royals and got a half dozen pictures. We built a full-page ad that ran in *TV Week*. At this point, Expo was just a few months away and we hadn't put anything else in place to ensure that the project would work out, but we asked readers to send in $9.95 with their order for the commemorative magazine. Not long after, I had a thousand cheques sitting on my desk, but the finance people were still telling me that it wasn't enough. So we ran the ad a few more times and got another thousand cheques. At which point I told the finance people, "Either we send these cheques back or we deposit the cheques and commit to the project."

We put the money in the bank and the rest is Canada Wide history. Visitors and locals alike loved the commemorative magazines and they snapped them up. By the end of Expo, we had sold tens of thousands of copies and it was a very profitable venture for my company.

But that wasn't the end of the line for this particular idea.

A short time later, my mentor Ray Addington mentioned to me that Galen Weston had asked him to help raise money for the Pearson College of the Pacific in Victoria, which is a member of United Colleges. Ray asked me if I had any ideas on what sort of appeal might create some interest.

"Isn't Prince Charles currently the president of that group of colleges?" I asked Ray. He confirmed that indeed he was.

"I have just the thing for you then," I told him. "What do you think about asking the Prince to write and sign a covering letter that we could insert into the commemorative magazine of his recent visit to Expo? We could print another 20,000 copies of the magazine, add the letter and sell them as a fundraiser for the college."

Ray was thrilled with the idea and we got down to business.

The Prince was more than happy to oblige for a cause that was very near and dear to him and when the campaign was over, we managed to raise a total of $70,000 for the college. Not bad, I'd say, for something that started out as "the worst idea" I'd ever presented to my financial team.

CHAPTER 27

"What we need are more people who specialize in the impossible."

— Theodore Roethke

Masterpiece Tool:
Emulate Success

Why is it that some people are infinitely more successful in business — and in life — than others? I believe all successful people share a few qualities that are timeless. One of these is the habit of observing what other successful people do, incorporating it into their own life and then repeating it often enough until it works for them.

Walt Disney was one such man who knew a thing or two about creating a successful enterprise. "You can dream, create, design and build the most wonderful place in the world, but it requires people to make the dream a reality," he said.

The Disney organization works very hard to meet the top three expectations that customers have when they visit a Disney theme park: for the park to be clean, friendly and fun. Every team member, from the CEO to the housekeepers in Disney resorts, knows these expectations and is empowered to make them happen. In fact, Disney was the very first company to open a corporate university where they could train employees to their own high standards.

Everything they teach is based on the following five secrets of Disney Success:

1. **Think tomorrow**. According to his brother and partner Roy Disney, Walt always operated on the theory of making today pay off tomorrow. When something didn't turn out quite as he expected, he would simply focus on tomorrow, come up with a new idea and keep moving forward. This philosophy got him through his greatest disappointments.

   In fact, even Mickey Mouse was a failure at first. That's because right at the time Walt was introducing his new character, a new technology emerged on the scene. That technology was sound and it ushered in the era of the talking picture. Not one to be left behind, Walt adopted the new technology and the third Mickey Mouse cartoon, *Steamboat Willie*, opened on November 18, 1928 as the first animated talkie. It was a huge hit.

2. **Strive for lasting quality**. It is well known that Walt Disney refused to release a film until it had the kind of quality he thought would last. In 1938, after six months had been spent working on the film *Pinocchio*, Walt suddenly suspended production saying that the film just didn't have heart. It wasn't until he found a solution in the character of Jiminy Cricket (with his colourful personality), that he allowed the film to be completed and released.

3. **Practically perfect in every way**. Walt Disney believed that if you were going to do a thing, you'd better do it well, even if it cost a lot more to do so. When the production of *Pinocchio* was finally completed, the film cost a whopping $2.6 million (Disney had made his first feature-length film, *Snow White*, for $1.5 million). However, Walt was not concerned. "If the show is good

enough, the public will pay us back for it," he said.

4. **Have stick-to-it-ivity**. Walt made this word up himself and it perfectly describes the trait that contributed the most to his success in life. When his feature film *Alice in Wonderland* flopped at the box office, its failure convinced Walt's brother Roy, who was in charge of the finances, that it was a bad time to use studio money to build a theme park. However, Walt was not to be deterred. The park had been his dream ever since his daughters were little and he wasn't going to let go of it. To hire a draftsman to lay out the plans for a theme park, he hawked his life insurance to raise $100,000 to pay for it out of his own pocket. In 1955 Disneyland opened in Anaheim, California.

5. **Have fun**. The focus of Walt Disney's entire career, and indeed his life, was to have fun and entertain people. From the time he first dreamed up Mickey Mouse to the creation of his masterpiece, the Disney empire, he never lost sight of his purpose. In fact, he once noticed a railroad conductor in Disneyland who was being curt with passengers. Seeing this he turned to an assistant and said, "Give that fellow a better understanding of the business we're in. If you can't cheer him up, he shouldn't be working here. We're selling happiness."

There is no doubt that Walt Disney knew the secrets to make dreams come true. His enduring masterpiece is that he was willing to share his secrets with the world.

———•◦•———

One of the most influential speakers in my career has been Nido Qubein, a Horatio Alger award-winner who, as I've mentioned before, came to the United States from Lebanon and despite the fact that he didn't speak one word of English, was determined to succeed.

He recently said to me, "In reality, you do become who you spend time with, so spending time with winners and learning the best habits that they have, and incorporating those habits into your own life is one of the success secrets that has brought me to where I am today."

The question is, "Who do you spend time with?"

———•—•———

"I am still learning."

— Michelangelo

———•—•———

Laurie Van Alstyne is the National Sales Manager for Travelers Financial Group. She sent me the following note of appreciation:

As often as you speak, you are no doubt inundated with thank-yous from persons whose lives you have touched. I am proud to add my name to this fortunate list. I have seen you speak three times now and it has always succeeded in refocusing me on what's important in life: honesty, integrity and passion. I have used your inspiration and motivation in mentoring my two daughters, myself and my co-workers. You instill belief and a reminder of the core values that sometimes get away from people, and again, I just want to thank you.

———•—•———

One of the keys to success is doing the things that failures don't like to do. If you are in sales, you should know that failures don't like:

1. Prospecting
2. Making calls
3. Selling
4. Working hard

———•◦•———

*A **MASTER KNOWS**: You can set yourself head and shoulders above the competition by simply focusing on giving customers what no one else is willing to give — good service.*

———•◦•———

Leonardo da Vinci was perhaps one of the most successful people in the history of the world, known for a diverse range of accomplishments, not the least among them being masterpieces of art like the Mona Lisa, anatomical studies of the human body and designs for inventions such as parachutes and flying machines. However, there were some projects that da Vinci never finished and the fact that he didn't was something that troubled him for the remainder of his life. On his deathbed in 1519, Leonardo expressed only two regrets about his life — that he was never able to fly and he never finished "his horse."

The project was a commission for his patron, Ludovico Sforza, the Duke of Milan. "Il Cavallo" was to be a magnificent 24-foot-tall bronze statue of a horse, the largest equine statue ever built. Leonardo began the project by constructing a full-scale clay model of his idyllic stallion in a vineyard. Unfortunately for him, the French army invaded Milan. As a result, the Duke ordered that the bronze that had been set aside for the statue be used to make a cannon and Leonardo's monumental clay cast of the horse was destroyed by the archers of the French army, who used it for target practice.

Leonardo fled Milan, the Duke fell and the French captured the city.

Although Leonardo died nearly 500 years ago, his dream of Il Cavallo did not. In 1977, United Airlines pilot and amateur Renaissance scholar Charles Dent read about the intriguing story of Leonardo and his horse in an issue of *National Geographic* magazine.

Filled with great enthusiasm and inspiration, Dent's instantaneous response to the story was, "Let's give Leonardo his horse." Realizing that this was no small undertaking, Dent sold his own art collection to support the project and then created a non-profit organization to continue raising funds. He also brought together a group of sculptors, friends, relatives, horse lovers and hundreds of enthusiasts who, after hearing the story, contributed time, effort and financial resources to help make Leonardo's dream come true.

Coincidentally, like Leonardo, Dent did not live to see his "crazy, romantic scheme" come to life. He died on Christmas Day in 1994, but by then the momentum behind the $6-million project to reconstruct the horse from Leonardo's sketches had gained so much momentum that it was unstoppable.

It is ironic that after Charlie Dent's death, his will (which was essentially a bequest to Il Cavallo) provided the substantial sum that took the model to the foundry in Beacon, New York, where it was to be enlarged to a colossal scale and cast in bronze.

On September 10, 1999, more than 500 years after the Duke of Milan and Leonardo had envisioned it, the completed 24-foot horse was unveiled to more than 1,000 spectators in Milan. It was presented as a gift to the people of Italy from the American people as a thank you for the treasures of the Renaissance, and also as a tribute to the marriage of scientific thinking and artistic creativity — two of Leonardo's greatest passions.

CHAPTER 28

*"My private measure of success is daily.
If this were to be the last day of my life, would
I be content with it? To live in a
harmonious balance of commitments
and pleasures is what I strive for."*

— Jane Rule

Masterpiece Tool:
Creating Balance in Your Life

When CNN asked Shelly Lazarus, Chairman and CEO of Ogilvy & Mather Worldwide, to share the golden rule that she lives by, she said quite simply, "Business can't trump happiness."

She went on to explain, "Unless you love your work, you won't find balance. How can you, if you resent the time away from family spent at a tedious job? I fell into a job and a company I loved. I never wanted to leave and never worried that my family suffered for it. Finding fulfilling work should be an early and deeply pursued part of everyone's career path. This may sound soft and mushy, but happy people are better for business. They are more creative and productive, they build environments where success is more likely and you have a much better chance of keeping your best players."

Former U.S. Secretary of State Colin Powell agrees. "Have fun in your command," he says. "Don't always run at a breakneck pace. Take leave when you've earned it. Spend time with your family and surround yourself with people who take their work seriously, but not themselves, those who work hard and play hard."

———•———

A MASTER KNOWS: Achievement and enjoyment are the front and back of the coin that depicts value in life. You can't have a worthwhile life with one and not the other, just as a coin that is stamped on just one side would not be legal tender. Trying to live a one-sided life is why so many "successful" people are not happy, or not nearly as happy as they should be.

———•———

If my kids have any positive memories, it will be that I've engineered holidays and weekends, planning some kind of trip, somewhere, on an annual basis for the last 30 years. We've done Hawaii, London and Toronto; we've been on cruises; attended concerts and plays; visited museums and amusement parks; participated in cultural events and festivals; we've even shopped until we dropped, and it has been one of the elements that has kept the five of us really tight for 30-plus years. We're not enmeshed, but we are a very close Legge family. They love it and I love it!

Even now that my youngest daughter Amanda is happily married, we still like to go on trips together. In 2004, Amanda and her husband Trevor came over for a Sunday dinner and announced that they were planning a trip to New York City. The entire family was around the dinner table at the time and so I said, "That's great, why don't we all go?"

So we did!

Once we had agreed on a weekend when everyone was free, we all started making plans about what we should and shouldn't do on our adventure to the Big Apple. With the airline tickets booked, the first objective was a hotel in Manhattan.

Thankfully, I had an ace up my sleeve to deal with the hotel challenge. One of the organizations I'm involved with here at home is the Vancouver Doorman's Association, which has an annual fundraising dinner for Grace McCarthy's CHILD Foundation. Each year, visiting doormen from Denver, Las Vegas, Toronto and New York come to this unique dinner, and for the last decade, John Cavalis (a doorman for 40 years at the Sheraton in Manhattan) has been among them.

Needless to say, relationships play an important part when you are looking for a deal on a hotel in Manhattan (and everyone you will meet in your lifetime, no matter their station in life, has clout within their own circle of influence). As it happened, John has the authority to put friends and family in the hotel at significantly reduced room rates, and based on our convivial relationship, he was more than happy to oblige the Legge family and we were thrilled.

If you don't know, this hotel is literally four blocks from Times Square and a block and a half away from the Ed Sullivan Theater, where *Late Night with David Letterman* is taped. In fact, a few years ago, I sent five senior managers to the Folio magazine conference and asked John if he could get tickets to the David Letterman show for them (one of the few things I didn't seem able to accomplish, despite my good looks and charm).

Although John wasn't able to get tickets for my managers to be in the studio audience (it was very short notice), he didn't let us down. Because he knew the caterer who served the crew of the show, he arranged for my four senior managers to substitute for the catering staff that day and bring in the sandwiches and coffee for the crew. Then, once they had completed their task, they could stay and watch the show. My staff were thrilled and they had a great time.

Now, back to the family weekend in New York.

We arrived at the hotel around midnight on a Thursday and as time was precious, everybody wanted to make the most of every moment. Given its proximity to the hotel, we decided that our first stop had to be the world-famous Carnegie Deli. So at midnight, we all marched over there and had world-famous corned beef on rye sandwiches with coleslaw and it was better than you can imagine.

Of course, any trip to New York has to include some serious shopping, although I still can't fathom why my children elected to take a four-hour round trip on the bus to New Jersey's outlet centre mall when everything they wanted was within mere blocks of our hotel. To make it even more challenging (a race against the clock), we had booked seats to see the play *Chicago* that evening. If you've ever been to New York, you can imagine the traffic jam they faced on the return trip into downtown New York on a Friday evening from Jersey.

When they finally got close, the bus dropped them off at Madison Square Gardens (which was 25 blocks from our hotel) and they ran the whole 25 blocks back to the hotel in the pouring rain so as not to be late for the play. We were relieved to see them come crashing through the door, dripping wet, with no time to spare.

We crammed as much as we possibly could into that weekend in New York, including a trip to the Metropolitan Museum, morning services at a Baptist Church and ice skating in Central Park. We bought stuff on the street — purses, belts, bags, scarves (all of them knock-offs) — we went to Chinatown, ate in lots of different restaurants and literally had the time of our lives!

We've been doing this for 30 years and it's something that we all look forward to and enjoy. I can hardly wait for the next adventure . . . wherever it might be.

———•·•———

A MASTER KNOWS: You can't be the wealthiest guy in the world and have no friends. You can't do so much for everyone else that you sacrifice your family or well-being. You need to include your spouse and your children in whatever is occupying the majority of your time and attention.

———•·•———

Here is a story from Heidi Dorman, Marketing Coordinator at Canada Wide, who found just what she was looking for hanging on the wall in our lobby.

I only had one semester left in the Marketing Management Program at BCIT and the majority of that term was to be completed doing an internship. The head of the Marketing Department suggested that a company called Canada Wide Magazines would be a good fit for me.

I went for an informational interview on December 20, 2004 to meet with Samantha Legge, the company's Director of Marketing. As I sat waiting for my interview, I could feel the excitement rising inside me. If all went well, this might turn into my place of employment after the internship. Of course, that wouldn't just depend on whether the job was suitable for my skills, it was also important to me to find a company that was in line with my values.

As I sat there awaiting my interview, I noticed that the company had framed a copy of both their Mission Statement and their core corporate values and put them on the wall in the lobby for everyone to see. I read through the Mission Statement and list of core values carefully and right then and there decided that if all of those ideals were actually realized in the day-to-day operations of this organization, then this was a company that I would want to work for.

The interview with Samantha went very well and I found myself interning with the company. During that time, I was impressed by the culture they had created for their employees and when my internship was over, I was lucky enough to transition smoothly into the position of Marketing Coordinator. When it comes to values, I can honestly say that this is a company that walks the talk and I am proud to walk in the door each morning knowing that I am working for a company that is not only very successful in terms of the bottom line, but also in terms of making a difference in the lives of its employees and the community as a whole.

Here is Canada Wide Magazine's "Mission Statement and Core Values," the document that Heidi saw on her first visit to the company.

Mission Statement
Our Mission is to be Western Canada's Dynamic Leader in the Magazine Publishing Industry.

Seven Core Values
- **Honesty** — Honesty and integrity in all of our business dealings, both inside Canada Wide and outside the company, is the cornerstone of our business.
- **Competency** — We are committed to encouraging, developing and maintaining the highest levels of professional expertise in every employee to ensure excellence in all

aspects of the products and services we provide.

- **Vision** — We are committed to keeping our eyes trained on the future and to encourage the sharing of new ideas among all of our employees.
- **Profitability** — We are committed to thoughtful planning and responsive management in all sectors of the company to ensure the company's ongoing financial success.
- **Customer Service** — We are committed to developing a thorough understanding of the unique needs of every client and to developing and delivering top-quality products that fully meet those needs.
- **Meaningful Employment with a Future** — We are committed to the growth and development of all of our employees and to ensuring their success and future within Canada Wide.
- **Community Involvement** — We are committed to supporting charitable endeavours and to putting our resources to work for the betterment of the community.

CHAPTER 29

"Responsibility is the price of greatness."
— Winston Churchill

Masterpiece Tool:
Taking Responsibility

Perhaps one of the hardest lessons that we all have to learn in life is that we are ultimately responsible for the choices we make and therefore also responsible for the eventual success or failure of all of our endeavours. This of course, reminds me of a story . . .

I was on a 30th-wedding anniversary cruise with my wife Kay. We had flown from Vancouver to London and then on to Istanbul where we spent a couple days seeing the sights. After visiting a number of ancient sites and buying the customary carpet, we boarded P&O's *Pacific Princess*, the original ship used in the *Love Boat* TV series, for a cruise to Athens, Rhodes, the Holy Land, Egypt and Rome.

Our first port of call was Athens where everyone was very excited to see the Parthenon. Along with all the other passengers, Kay and I disembarked from the ship to see the sights. I have to mention that the highlight for me wasn't the ancient ruins. Rather, it was the opportunity to climb up and stand atop Mars Hill where Paul from the *New Testament* stood so many centuries ago and welcomed the people to Athens.

The ship was scheduled to leave Athens for our next port of

call at 6 p.m. that evening. We got back to the ship on time and went to our cabin to get dressed for dinner. To our surprise, the ship did not leave port on schedule. In fact, when we sat down to eat at 7 p.m., we were still in port and also at 8 p.m. By 9 p.m., we had finished dinner and I said to Kay, "I'll bet you there's some sort of problem." At about 9:15, the captain came on the loudspeaker to inform us that we did in fact have a serious problem.

Two Filipino chefs from the ship had been caught smuggling drugs from Istanbul to Athens and were being detained by authorities. In fact, because of the seriousness of the offence, Greek officials had arrested the entire ship, including the crew and all 650 passengers onboard. We were subsequently stuck in Athens for six days and nights. After the sixth night, P&O cancelled the entire cruise and either flew passengers home or on to their next destination.

For us, and I'm sure the rest of the passengers, Princess Cruises also refunded the entire cruise price, the return airfare from Vancouver to Istanbul and other incidental expenses. Considering the fact that approximately 80 per cent of their passengers are repeat travellers, from a customer-service point of view, I agree that it was absolutely the right thing for the company to do.

As for the Filipino chefs, I think they offer a great lesson about responsibility for all of us. Our life is a blank canvas and we are the painters. We can either choose to paint a masterpiece . . . or we can choose to spend the next 25 years in a jail in Greece.

———•+•———

A MASTER KNOWS: Personal responsibility is nothing other than the freedom to create our own lives. We are the architects of our success and when we blame others, we give away our power.

———•+•———

Golf is a great game for many reasons, not the least of which is the fact that it relies on the individual to take responsibility for his or her actions. Legendary golfer Jack Nicklaus recently played his last British Open Championship at St. Andrews in Scotland.

Throughout his career, Nicklaus has been a hero and inspiration to many and at all times a gentleman of the highest order. Today, he is passing along the values that every golfer is expected to live by to young people through an organization he founded called First Tee. Here then are the nine core values that I think apply equally well to business and life as they do to golf. I have printed them in a previous book, but I think they bear repeating:

1. *Honesty* — Golf is unique from other sports in that players regularly call penalties on themselves.

2. *Integrity* — Golf is a game of honesty, etiquette and composure. You are responsible for your actions and conduct at all times, no matter whether you are winning or losing.

3. *Sportsmanship* — You must know and abide by the rules of golf and conduct yourself in a respectable manner.

4. *Respect* — It is important to respect yourself, your partners, opponents and the course plus the game's honour and traditions.

5. *Confidence* — Confidence plays a key role in the level of play you achieve.

6. *Responsibility* — You are responsible for yourself and your actions on the course. You must:
   - Keep score
   - Repair divots
   - Rake bunkers
   - Repair ball marks
   - Keep up with the pace of play

7. *Perseverance* — To succeed in golf, you must learn to persevere through bad breaks and your own mistakes.

8. *Courtesy* — Begin and end play with a handshake. Show courtesy by remaining still and quiet during other players' shots.

9. *Judgment* — Good judgment comes into play when deciding strategy and club selection as well as abiding by etiquette.

"The man who complains about the way the ball bounces is likely to be the one who dropped it."

— Lou Holtz

It's sometimes difficult to watch our children learn lessons of responsibility the hard way (just as we did before them), but when they later grow up to be strong, capable adults, we know it was all worthwhile. As with most such stories, the following one took place when my daughter was in her teens and testing the boundaries of her independence.

My middle daughter Rebecca once worked at a Red Robin restaurant and I wish to make it clear at the outset of this story that Rebecca had never been in any trouble with us for any infractions or broken rules whatsoever.

It was a typical Friday night and Rebecca took Kay's car to work where her normal time for finishing was midnight. Although we lived literally five minutes from the Red Robin location (and we really did want to give all of our children a sense of independence), as parents we also worried about their safety and so we had always insisted that the manager walk Rebecca through the parking lot to her car when she worked an evening shift.

On this night, Rebecca did not return home at her usual time and by 1 a.m., when there was still no sign of Rebecca, we telephoned the restaurant manager whom we knew would still be working. He told us that yes, he had walked Rebecca to the car, but as it was a very slow night she had left work at 10 p.m.

At 2:30 in the morning, Rebecca finally walked in the door. Having waited up for so long, my first question was, of course, "What happened? Why are you are so late?"

Rebecca looked at me and responded matter of factly, "Oh Dad, it was a very busy night at the restaurant. I stayed late to help clean up and the manager still walked me to the car. I guess I lost track of time."

Rebecca's younger sister Amanda, who was sitting on the floor watching all of this unfold, fixed her sister with a look and began shaking her head. "You're just digging yourself deeper and deeper, Rebecca," she said. "Mom and Dad know."

CHAPTER 30

"Life is too short to eat Brussels sprouts."

— Samantha Legge

Masterpiece Tool:
Focus on What is Important

When my three girls were young children, my wife Kay and I made a point of introducing them to many different kinds of food, including vegetables. While we didn't believe in forcing the girls to eat foods that they really didn't like, our philosophy was that you at least had to try a few mouthfuls in order to make up your mind.

So it was that we attempted to get Samantha to eat Brussels sprouts one evening at Sunday dinner. As usual, when dinner was put on the table, Kay served up a small portion of vegetables to each of the children. Unfortunately for Samantha, when the Brussels sprouts landed on her plate, it was most definitely not love at first sight. As dinner progressed, she managed to eat around the offending vegetables and thinking herself finished, asked if she could be excused from the table.

"No, you may not," Kay said firmly, looking at the untouched vegetables on Samantha's plate. "You haven't even tried the Brussels sprouts."

"I don't want to try them," said Samantha. "I already know that I don't like them."

Not one to give in easily, Kay held her ground. "When you've finished what's on your plate, you may be excused," she told Samantha.

After sitting at the table, glaring at the two lonely Brussels sprouts on her plate for the better part of a half hour, Samantha decided to take a different tack and negotiate with her mother (a tactic I would highly recommend to any child in a similar situation).

"If I eat these two Brussels sprouts," she propositioned. "Do you promise that you will never make me eat Brussels sprouts again as long as I live?"

"Absolutely," Kay agreed. "As long as you at least try them."

Looking as if a life sentence had suddenly been lifted from her head, Samantha quickly ate the vegetables and excused herself from the table.

While I was writing this book, I happened to mention to Samantha that I was thinking of including the story about her and the Brussels sprouts in a chapter that would focus on paying attention to the things that are important in your life. In response, she turned to me and said, "Yeah, Dad, that would make a good chapter. After all, life is too short to eat Brussels sprouts. "

Masterpieces don't happen overnight and sadly, sometimes they don't happen at all. In Jerusalem, there are two museums side by side called Yad Vashem. The first of the two deals with the rise of Hitler and Nazism, the persecution of the Jews and the brutal reality of the concentration camps. It addresses this horrific period of our history in a vivid and graphic manner, in sharp contrast to the children's museum right next door. Here, you enter the museum by going underground about 10 feet. Once you are inside and have adjusted your eyes to the dark, all you see are simulated stars in the sky. As you walk through this museum, all you hear are a man's voice and a woman's voice in turn speaking out the name, age and country of a child who lost his or her life during the Holocaust, at the rate of about one name every 20 or 30 seconds. It takes about 10 minutes to travel through the museum. As you leave, you are told that they could keep up the recitation of names for two years without saying the same name twice.

Those children never had an opportunity to make a masterpiece out of their lives. The children's museum reminded me about how important it is to help people to be the best that they can be. In most cases, it takes years of hard work to obtain the knowledge and skills you need to begin your masterpiece and then many more years of applying yourself to your chosen craft — but it all begins with someone giving you the chance to prove yourself.

Here is a letter from one such young man who came to intern with my company last summer. Despite a physical disability that required him to walk using crutches, Aaron Broverman made the long trip to our offices each day to work in our editorial department and hone his writing skills.

Dear Peter,

Working for your company, Canada Wide, and with the TV Week *team has been amazing these last two months. I learned a lot about my chosen field and feel this experience will only further my development as a journalist. Thank you for your support, encouragement and kind words about my positive attitude and strong work ethic. It all means a lot to me coming from you, especially when you could've kept walking and didn't have to say anything. Thank you again. I feel there is nowhere to go from here but forward and I know we'll meet again.*

Sincerely,

Aaron Broverman

TV Week *intern, July & August 2005*

———•————

A MASTER KNOWS: Truly successful people don't waste time making excuses; they find a way to do what they love!

———•————

There is an amusing story about the famous painter Pablo Picasso who, by the way, was the first living artist ever to be exhibited at the Louvre Museum in Paris.

One day Picasso was riding on the train and a gentleman sitting next to him suddenly turned and addressed him, asking in a pointed way, "Why don't you create paintings that look realistic — just like your subject?" To demonstrate what he meant, the man reached into his pocketbook and pulled out a photograph of his wife to show to Picasso.

Picasso looked at the picture and then replied, "She's awfully small and flat."

As the son of an art teacher, Picasso discovered his passion for painting at a very early age. He exhibited his first paintings in Barcelona at the age of 12 and went on to create many master-pieces. Picasso continued to pursue his life's passion right up until his death in 1973 at the age of 91. During his lifetime, he is said to have produced approximately 20,000 paintings, sculptures and drawings. The sculptor Henry Moore once called Picasso one of the most "naturally gifted" artists since Raphael.

———•————

Not all masters create works of art that can be hung on a museum wall. I was on a business trip to England with my daughter Rebecca and we found ourselves enjoying a meal in the oldest restaurant in London. Established in 1798, this venerable dining room is renowned not only for its food but also for the cavalcade of literary giants who have made it their second home through the years. The restaurant has been the favourite haunt of such legendary writers as Charles Dickens, William Makepeace Thackeray, John Galsworthy and H.G. Wells, as well as a comfortable respite for British royalty.

In the more than 200 years since it was founded, spanning the reign of nine monarchs, this restaurant has been owned by only three families. Today it seats 200 guests on three floors, employs 100 staff and serves an average of 500 people a day — that's 150,000 customers a year.

We had to find out how this business has not only survived, but thrived, for all this time. So we asked the senior manager, Edward Donnelly, to share the secret to the longevity and success of this fine, old business.

The restaurant, Donnelly explained, has only three rules — rules from which it never deviates:

Rule 1: Serve and specialize in a niche market — game meats.

Rule 2: Take game meats seriously at all times.

Rule 3: Adapt easily — no hierarchy.

These are the rules. So, what is the name of this fantastic restaurant? You guessed it. It's called Rules!

Recently, my wife Kay and I were having dinner at another restaurant right here in Vancouver with Joe and Rosalie Segal. The restaurant is called Le Crocodile. Although I had never been there before, I had heard plenty about the food from friends and associates and we were looking forward to a sumptuous dinner based on the establishment's legendary reputation.

We were not disappointed.

As we sat talking after the meal, we got on the topic of what makes a restaurant successful and I asked the maître d' to tell me about the history of the restaurant. She informed me that the 85-seat restaurant was opened more than 20 years ago as a means for owner/chef Michel Jacob to express his passion for French cuisine.

She proceeded to tell me that in September 2005, Michel won a very prestigious French culinary award. The award included a prize of $5,000, but there was one very interesting stipulation attached. The prize money was not meant for the winner's use; Michel was required to give the money to another restaurant of his choosing, to help in its development.

Michel chose to give the $5,000 to The Pear Tree Restaurant in Burnaby, which is operated by Scott Jaeger, a fellow owner/chef who has been making a name for himself in culinary circles.

I think this type of award is a great concept that could be applied to any industry, even my own of magazine publishing. When I look at how many new magazines struggle in their first few years of operation, I can see how the money could really help a new title to get established in its niche market.

Before we left the restaurant, I asked the maître d' to tell me what three things make Le Crocodile successful. Here is what she told me:

1. Consistent food preparation.
2. Little or no change to the menu.
3. Everything we do is done with passion.

Thinking back to my conversation with the senior manager of Rules Restaurant in London, I can see a lot of similarities between these two fine establishments and their approach to business. Although they are in different countries, on different continents, they are essentially focusing on the same standards of excellence, and when you stop to think about it, those could be applied to any business.

To end this chapter, I would like to share with you a very personal story about a revelation that took me a lot of soul-searching to come to terms with.

I was with my wife and three children on our annual family holiday in Hawaii when the kids were in their teens. Following two glorious weeks of surfing, shopping and enjoying the sun and sand, we headed out to the Honolulu International Airport to board a Canadian Airlines DC 10 for the five-and-a-half-hour flight home to Vancouver.

As the plane left the ground, it banked over Waikiki Beach giving us one last glimpse of the paradise we had enjoyed for the past two weeks before it started to climb up over Diamond Head and head northwards towards Vancouver. As the wheels tucked up under the plane, a very unusual noise could be heard in the cabin and I half expected to hear the captain make an announcement that we would have to turn back due to mechanical difficulties. However, nothing was said by the captain or crew about a problem, so I settled in for the duration.

In my mind, the best flights are the uneventful ones and this flight was shaping up to be one of them . . . that is, until we were on our approach into Vancouver and the pilot attempted to put the landing gear down, at which point we heard a noticeable bang.

It was now approaching midnight, and about three-quarters of the way into our descent, the captain suddenly aborted the landing and resumed altitude, flying towards Victoria. He then banked around and flew towards Mission to make another approach to land. During this time, he announced to the passengers that there was a potential problem with the landing gear. He also said that he had been instructed by the control tower to fly as low as possible over the runway so that the ground crew could visually check to see if the wheels were down.

It was a clear night as we approached the runway for the fly-over and I remember seeing dozens of red flashing lights as we swooped over the tarmac. As we banked and went around one more time, the pilot told us that the landing gear did appear to be down and he was going to attempt a landing. The attendants on the flight instructed us to assume the brace position on the captain's command.

You can only imagine the ideas that were running through my head at that moment. I remember it only as one of the most horrific 20 minutes of my life. I began to pray and what shocked me and subsequently embarrassed me was the realization that in that terrible moment I didn't pray for the captain or the crew, I didn't pray for my three children or even my wife . . . but I did pray for myself.

After the plane had landed and we were taxiing to the terminal, one of my daughters, who was sitting right behind me, touched me on the shoulder and said, "Hey, Dad, just think of the story you'll have to tell about this."

"Yeah, it would make some story," I thought to myself. "A story about just how selfish I really am."

I thought about that experience for a long time and it bothered me. I wondered what it said about me as a father and husband. I worried that I must be a terribly selfish, awful human being who only cared for himself. I wondered if there was another, darker side of myself that I was hiding from my family, but also from myself.

I had always thought of myself as a kind, caring person who put the security of my wife and certainly my children before my own. How could I be so selfish?

After a good deal of soul-searching, I talked to my wife about the situation and asked her what she thought it said about me.

"Well, Peter, we've been together for very nearly all of our adult life and like most people, we've experienced some ups and downs and faced some difficulties," she said. "In all that time, you've never shown anything but kindness, caring and concern for your parents, your colleagues, your friends and most of all for me and our three daughters. So the only thing I think it says about you, my dear, is that you are human."

Looking back now, I don't mind admitting the thoughts that I had on that airplane. While the experience showed me just how fallible I am, it also taught me something about the important difference between the thoughts that may go through my mind and the actions that I take in the world. While I may not always be able to control my thoughts, I certainly can choose how I treat the people around me, how I run my business, how I take part in my community and how I live out my life in the world . . . and that's what is really important in the end.

EPILOGUE

Ready or Not

Excerpted from a piece written by Michael Josephson

Ready or not, someday this life will all come to an end. There will be no more sunrises, no minutes, hours or days. All the things you collected, whether treasured or forgotten, will pass to someone else.

Your wealth, fame and temporal power will shrivel to irrelevance. It will not matter what you owned or what you were owed.

Your grudges, resentments, frustrations and jealousies will finally disappear. So too, your hopes, ambitions, plans and to-do lists will all expire.

The wins and losses that once seemed so important will fade away. It won't matter where you came from or on which side of the tracks you lived. At the end it won't matter whether you were beautiful or brilliant and even your gender and skin colour will be irrelevant.

So what will matter? How will the value of your days be measured?

What will matter is not what you bought but what you built; not what you got, but what you gave.

What will matter is not your success, but your significance.

What will matter is not what you learned, but what you taught.

What will matter is every act of integrity, compassion, courage or sacrifice that enriched, empowered or encouraged others to emulate your example.

What will matter is not your competence, but your character.

What will matter is not how many people you knew, but how many will feel a lasting loss when you are gone.

What will matter is not your memories, but the memories that live on with those who loved you.

What will matter is how long you will be remembered, by whom and for what.

Living a life that matters doesn't happen by accident.

It's not a matter of circumstance, but of choice.

It is up to you to choose wisely.

AFTERWORD

This past Christmas, my youngest daughter Amanda and her husband Trevor added to my library at home a great book written by U.S. Senator John McCain, entitled *Character is Destiny*.

The book uses as examples real people who demonstrate the many essential character traits that can move us towards a life of significance, with values such as honesty, respect, loyalty, dignity, diligence, responsibility, courage, compassion, resilience, hopefulness, courtesy, fairness, generosity, humility, forgiveness, discernment, enthusiasm and excellence.

Names you would expect in a book of this nature include Mahatma Gandhi, Sir Winston Churchill, Dr. Viktor Frankl, Joan of Arc, Canadian hero General Romeo Dallaire (with whom I had the distinct privilege of sharing the platform at a Canadian Red Cross *Power of Humanity* Awards Dinner), U.S. basketball coach John Wooden, Abraham Lincoln, Queen Elizabeth I, Mother Teresa, Dwight Eisenhower, George Washington, Lord Nelson and many other names from the annals of history.

The 300-page book devotes about four or five pages to how each person used his or her own unique talents to make a masterpiece of his or her life, and I was happy to find so many chapters highlighting stories about the accomplishments of several individuals whom I had not heard about (you will have to buy the book for yourself to find out who they are). Reading these chapters convinced me of the fact that when we are born, our life truly is a blank canvas ready to be painted into a masterpiece, and that masterpiece can take many forms.

Eric Hoffer, the great 20th-century thinker who considered himself a longshoreman, not a philosopher, is a good example of this. A man with no formal schooling, he spent much of his childhood in blindness, a fact that left him facing a life of manual labour. Believing in his own capacity to learn, Hoffer educated himself by reading the great books of the world as he supported himself as a migratory worker. Based on his reading, Hoffer developed ideas and theories about human behaviour that he put into books such as *The True Believer: Thoughts on the Nature of Mass Movements,* where he hypothesized that mass movements such as the one led by the Nazis in Germany were an outlet for people whose individual significance is meagre in the eyes of the world and — more importantly — in their own eyes. "The less justified a man is in claiming excellence for his own self, the more ready he is to claim all excellence for his nation, his religion, his race or his holy cause," stated Hoffer.

Hoffer also believed strongly that we need to take responsibility for creating our own masterpiece. In *The Passionate State of Mind* he wrote, "There are many who find a good alibi far more attractive than an achievement. For an achievement does not settle anything permanently. We still have to prove our worth anew each day: we have to prove that we are as good today as we were yesterday. But when we have a valid alibi for not achieving anything, we are fixed, so to speak, for life."

Critics and scholars describe Hoffer's work as some of the most insightful commentary on modern society and trends in the world. Shortly before his death, Hoffer was awarded the Medal of Freedom by then-U.S. president Ronald Reagan.

Another example is the story of Edith Cavell, a dedicated British nurse in the First World War who gave her life to save others. During the war, Cavell was working at a Red Cross hospital for Allied soldiers in German-occupied Belgium where she treated the soldiers and then helped them to escape. In 1915, she was arrested and charged with having aided in the escape of more than 200 soldiers. Cavell refused to lie to save her life and so she was convicted and sentenced to death. She was executed by firing squad on October 12, 1915. Cavell's heroism sparked a flood of volunteers to line up at recruiting stations in England, Canada, Australia and other parts of the British Empire. It also put pressure on the U.S. to join the war against Germany. The name of Edith Cavell continues to live on in many ways today; a nursing school in Brussels bears her name, and a statue of her stands in Trafalgar Square in London. Even a peak in Alberta's Jasper National Park has been christened Mount Edith Cavell.

As our own lives progress and our masterpiece begins to take shape, the development of character should be extremely high on our list. Take the time to ask yourself, "What kind of a masterpiece am I creating and what does it reflect about my character?" Understand that while your circumstances may determine the colours that you have to work with, the choices that you make day to day are in fact the brushstrokes that will define what your masterpiece looks like on the canvas.

Recently, I met a legend of Canada's national game, hockey. One of the country's master hockey players is NHL Hall of Fame inductee Lanny McDonald, whose 16-year NHL career included time with the Toronto Maple Leafs, the Colorado Rockies and seven-and-a-half years with the Calgary Flames. He and I were on the same convention program as speakers and he ended his presentation with a quote that really inspired me.

*"Every job is a self-portrait of the person who did it.
So autograph your work with excellence."*

I believe this truly is the key to making your life a masterpiece. Autograph everything you do with excellence. Commit today to take control of your canvas of life and create the masterpiece you were meant to be. Good luck, Godspeed and don't forget to send me an invitation to the big opening.

"The best preparation for tomorrow is to do today's work superbly well."

— Sir William Osler

ABOUT THE AUTHOR

Dr. Peter Legge, LL.D (HON) • CSP • CPAE

Peter Legge is President and CEO of Canada Wide Magazines & Communications Ltd., the largest independently owned publishing company in Western Canada, controlling a network of 36 magazines across the country with over $25 million in sales annually.

In addition, Peter travels the world as a motivational speaker, accepting more than 100 assignments each year from clients who know that when he speaks, his words will be a catalyst for positive change. He has received the prestigious Golden Gavel Award from Toastmasters International and was voted "Top Speaker in North America," in company with Dr. Robert Schuller and Stephen Covey. Peter has also been inducted into the Speakers Hall of Fame by both the National Speakers Association and the Canadian Association of Professional Speakers.

Peter is tireless in his commitments to many worthwhile organizations. As co-host of the annual Variety The Children's Charity Telethon for more than 29 years, he has assisted in raising more than $120 million for the charity. He is also an International Ambassador of Variety International.

His efforts have not gone unnoticed. Among his many honours, Peter has received the Golden Heart Award from the Variety Club and has been invested into the Venerable Order of St. John of Jerusalem, where he was recently promoted to Commander.

He has been awarded the Order of the Red Cross and named Citizen of the Year for his commitment to the community. Simon Fraser University recently honoured him with an Honorary Doctor of Laws Degree, and he is a past Chair of the Vancouver Board of Trade.

He is the recipient of the Nido Qubein Philanthropy Award presented to him at the NSA Convention in Atlanta in July 2005.

In April of this year, Sales and Marketing Executives International awarded Peter with the 2006 Ambassador of Free Enterprise in Dallas, Texas.

Peter is also the author of eight previous books that have inspired thousands of readers the world over with their powerful motivating messages. In all that he has achieved, Peter attributes his success to four factors: persistence, patience, a positive attitude and passion.

To contact Peter Legge, write to:
Peter Legge Management Company,
4180 Lougheed Highway, 4th Floor
Burnaby, B.C. V5C 6A7 Canada
Telephone: 604-299-7311
E-mail plegge@canadawide.com
Website: www.peterlegge.com

ORDER FORM

No	Description	Qty	Price	Total
B100	The Runway of Life *Hard Cover*		29.95 CDN 25.95 U.S.	
B101	If Only I'd Said That: Vol. II *Hard Cover*		29.95 CDN 25.95 U.S.	
B102	Who Dares Wins *Hard Cover*		29.95 CDN 25.95 U.S.	
B103	If Only I'd Said That: Vol. I *Hard Cover*		29.95 CDN 25.95 U.S.	
B104	If Only I'd Said That: Vol. III *Hard Cover*		29.95 CDN 25.95 U.S.	
B105	97 Tips on Customer Service* *Booklet*		4.97 CDN 3.97 U.S.	
B106	97 Tips to Jump-start Your Career* *Booklet*		4.97 CDN 3.97 U.S.	
	CDs & Videotapes			
V101	How To Soar With The Eagles* (90 mins.)		30.00 CDN 25.00 U.S.	
CD	The Runway of Life (60 mins.)		20.00 CDN 15.00 U.S.	
	Subtotal			
	Shipping and handling		5.00 CDN 3.00 U.S.	
	Subtotal			
	Canadian Residents add 7% GST			
	BC Residents Add 7% PST *(videotapes & booklets only)			
	TOTAL			

PAYMENT

☐ Cheque payable to Peter Legge Management Co. Ltd.

☐ Please charge $_____ to my MasterCard/Visa (CIRCLE ONE)

CC# _____Expiry Date_____

Signature _____

Please send my order to: (PLEASE PRINT)

Name_____Tel_____

Address_____

City_____Prov/State _____Postal/Zip_____

Peter Legge Management Co. Ltd., 4th Floor, 4180 Lougheed Hwy., Burnaby, B.C. V5C 6A7 Canada

For faster service FAX your credit card order to (604) 299-9188 or call (604) 299-7311
or order online www.peterlegge.com